Literary Reviews
And Criticisms

Dedicated
to
Charles F. Johnson, L.H.D.

Literary Reviews And Criticisms

By

Prosser Hall Frye

Essay Index Reprint Series

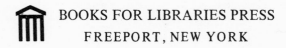 BOOKS FOR LIBRARIES PRESS
FREEPORT, NEW YORK

First Published 1908
Reprinted 1968

LIBRARY OF CONGRESS CATALOG CARD NUMBER:
68-8462

NOTE.

My acknowledgments are due the *Evening Post*, the *Bookman*, and the *Independent* for permission to reprint several of these pieces which appeared originally in their columns.

CONTENTS

Contents

Literary Reviews and Criticisms

LITERARY REVIEWS
AND CRITICISMS

THE ELIZABETHAN SONNET

E VERYBODY knows that Shakespeare wrote
sonnets; but it is not so generally understood how thoroughly the sonnet was a matter
of fashion in Shakespeare's day. Some notion
of its vogue in those times may be derived from
the fact that during the sixteenth century,
so it has been calculated, there were more than
300,000 sonnets produced in Western Europe.
These sonnets, particularly those of an amorous
nature, were often gathered into collections
or "sequences" and were dubbed with the
poetic pseudonyms of the inexpressive she's
who were their putative inspirers, and who were,
in fact, often saluted by their adorers as so
many tenth Muses. Of such collections the
present reissue of Arber's *English Garner* [1]

[1] *Elizabethan Sonnets.* With an Introduction by
Sidney Lee. 2 vols. New York: E. P. Dutton & Co.

I

contains fifteen examples, comprising those of Sidney, Drayton, Spenser, Daniel—in short, representing a large and by all odds the most important part of the sonneteering activity during the Elizabethan period, exclusive of Shakespeare's.

Such is the character of the book. And as it is now one of the most convenient sources for the study of this particular product, it is too bad that the text, which is virtually Arber's with the insertion of some additional matter, should not have been thoroughly revised. In some of the additions, for instance, an old spelling is retained after the present fashion, while in others it has suffered modernisation. Sometimes the syllabic *-ed* is indicated, sometimes not. The punctuation too ought to have been thoroughly overhauled. And it is to be wished that some one had taken the trouble to provide the *Diana* with a specification of Constable's contributions.

But these are minor matters after all and need not detain us. The most noteworthy part of the whole performance is the general introduction by Mr. Sidney Lee, who undertakes to assign the Elizabethan love-sonnet to its proper niche in the gallery of comparative literature. In order to indicate intelligibly what he has done, however, it will be necessary to explain briefly the nature of the collection.

What must strike the general reader most forcibly in looking over these sonnets—for with many of them reading is an impossible operation—is their wretchedness from the modern literary point of view. Historically and relatively they may be of some interest and importance; artistically and absolutely—if it is permissible to speak of an absolute in such affairs—they are of little or none either in matter or manner. Of course it is hardly to be expected of Elizabethan poetry, as a whole, that it should display the high and exquisite finish which we regard nowadays as indispensable to verse, particularly to such a kind of verse as the sonnet, Outside of the drama and some short snatches of simple song—and even here felicity seems often a matter of accident—there was, with few exceptions, no mastery of versification at this time, no certain and assured craftsmanship, such as begins to appear a little later with Drummond of Hawthornden. It is from Ben Jonson that this new idea of art, as a controlled and conscious workmanship distinct from inspiration and ancillary to it, actually emanates. But when Ben Jonson himself ventures outside of his province and undertakes to turn Horace into English rhymes, what a mess he makes of it! While Donne himself, the most remarkable poet between Jonson and Milton, is no very sure hand even with his own couplets. For a regular and masterful technique, then, we are not to look to this period. And especially in the case of these sonnets it is evident on the face of it that the writers are dealing with a form and a versification which, for some reason or other, they have acquired only very imperfectly and which in spite of their efforts still remains strange and foreign-seeming. In the mass their work, judge it by what standard you will, is exceedingly crude and ungainly, marked by lapses of taste and by discordant notes of all kinds, by violent wrenchings and inversions of sense and construction, and by a pathetic powerlessness to marry ictus and accent or to force recalcitrant rhymes into their proper places.

Now and then, to be sure, as might be expected, the gloom is relieved by a few flashes of that brilliant, if fitful, lightning which was at this very time playing about the contemporary drama:

"Plain patched experience, the unlettered's guide,"

or

"From looking on the earth whence she was born
Her mind remember'th her mortality,"

or again

"The light-foot lackey that runs post by death."

But such picturesque touches, such sultry gleams of Elizabethan spirit, are exceptional. And in general, it must be acknowledged, one has to grub pretty industriously to find anything worth while. The last advice the writers have thought of following, is that of Sidney's muse, "Look in thy heart and write." They present love, not as it is naturally seen by the individual or yet by humanity, but as an arbitrary and invariable convention. Their conception is inevitably composed of two main features: the lover's constancy and desperation, and his mistress's surpassing beauty and coldness. She has plundered the flower gardens of their sweets, the mines of Ophir and Ind of their treasures, Olympus of its perfections. Her cheek puts the roses to shame, her hand the lilies; her teeth are pearls, her eyes suns; she is lovely, not as Venus, who was rather too eligible a deity for our sonneteers, but as Juno, as wise as Minerva, as chaste as Diana, after whose example she delights to hound her lover to death, Actæon-like, with his own thoughts. As for that unfortunate gentleman himself, he spends his time in lamentation and weeping, when he is not inditing of canzones to his lady; he tosses nightly on a sleepless pillow; in the course of a little time his tears form a fountain by which he sits complaining to Echo, occasionally rousing to arbitrate between his eyes and heart while they dispute whether of the twain is guilty of first admitting love. And all this ingenious nonsense is further exaggerated and dilated by every imaginable sort of conceit, quirk, and oddity. Of the genealogy of Pain, for example, we are informed that he is child to Curse, foster-child to Human Weakness, brother to Woe, father to Complaint, and a guest of Constraint. One thing alone does the reader seldom or never meet with—the thrill of a genuine feeling or the warm pervasive aura of a real personality. It would appear as though these poetasters had deliberately selected some lady of their acquaintance, the more distant the better, and had proceeded to make up on her their literary exercises in accordance with the invariable prescription. In fact Giles Fletcher, author of *Licia*, admits that for once there is no woman in the case at all—or rather that she is a mere Platonic phantom, a kind of allegorised idea. In one sense, indeed, the writers may be said to have had a kind of basis of fact. Undoubtedly they turned to account such general incidents of their daily experience as were suggestive and could be readily poetised to fit the form. But the basis is always trivial. The main thing was the elaboration of the conventional pattern with which it was to be overlaid. And with the exception of Shakespeare, whose actuality

is unmistakable, their final impression is of
utter airiness and insubstantiality.

To this general run of mediocrity or
worse, as we should now reckon it, there
are naturally some exceptions. Principal
among such are Sidney's "With how sad
steps, O moon!" "Come, sleep, O sleep!"
and "Leave me, O Love!"; Daniel's "Care-
charmer sleep"; Spenser's "One day I wrote
her name upon the sand"; and Drayton's
exquisite "Since there's no help, come, let us
kiss and part," certainly the gem of the collection though it belongs in reality to a later
period. Most of these are well known or are
to be found in the "Golden Treasury." For
this reason it will be better to quote a sonnet — Barnes's — which is less familiar but
well worth reading as an illustration of their
higher reaches.

Ah, sweet Content! where is thy mild abode?
  Is it with shepherds and light-hearted Swains,
Which sing upon the downs and pipe abroad,
  Tending their flocks and cattle on the plains?
Ah, sweet Content! where dost thou safely rest?
  In heaven with angels? Which the praises sing
Of him that made and rules at his behest,
  The minds and hearts of every living thing.
Ah, sweet Content! where doth thine harbour hold ?
  Is it in churches with religious men,
Which please the gods with prayers manifold;
  And in their studies meditate it then?

Whether dost thou in heaven or earth appear;
Be where thou wilt !   Thou wilt not harbour here !
Barnes: *Parthenophil and Parthenope*, lxvi.

But such exceptions as this are very rare indeed—
and as for the rest they are essentially as has been
described.

At first thought there is something very
curious, almost disconcerting, about this sterility
in an age that we have been accustomed to
prefer before all others for its spontaneity,
imagination, and fire. Half a dozen good sonnets
—the list was nearly exhaustive—out of a
thousand; and it is difficult to pick up a play
of the time without finding more than one
evidence of great, if irregular, power! What,
then, is the explanation of this anomaly? As a
matter of fact, no serious answer to this question
has ever been attempted—possibly the question itself could not have been intelligently
propounded—before Mr. Lee's introductory
essay to these volumes. Of his solution—or
rather of the solution which suffers itself to be
drawn from his essay—the substance may be
briefly explained as follows:

It is hardly necessary to repeat that the
sonnet was introduced into England for the
first time about the middle of the sixteenth
century by Wyatt and Surrey, who had it
themselves from Petrarch, the head and front
of all sonneteering. But it was not exactly

in continuation of this original impulse that the
great flood of Elizabethan sonnet literature
began to rise in 1591. By that time the sonnet
was the rage throughout Europe, not only in
Italy, the land of its birth, but also in France,
where it had been domesticated by the *Pléiade*,
a group of writers devoted to the importation
of Italian literature, among whom Ronsard
is the most prominent. And it was from this
secondary or derivative source, this cistern
or reservoir, that the sonneteers of Elizabeth
pumped their supplies. The best of them,
such men as Sidney and Spenser, were, to be
sure, acquainted with Italian literature at
first hand. But even they were indebted in
great measure to the French, whereas the
feebler run of versifiers had frequently no other
support except their English contemporaries.
Nor was this debt in any case merely formal or
confined to the vague sphere of poetic influence
or inspiration. Not only is the whole conception
of the *genre* borrowed, but its *procédés* and execution are appropriated as well. The same
ideas and notions, the same conceits and figures,
the same individual features, recur through the
entire lineage, Italian, French, and English.
Even the vacuous idealism is a remote echo
of Petrarchian Platonism. In short, to cut down
a long story, the English sonnet is not only a
fad and liable to all the abuses of an artificial

fashion, it is also a *rechauffé*, a mere imitation
of an imitation, even a line-for-line translation
of foreign models, not particularly consonant,
it may be added, with the English genius. Of
this fact there can be no reasonable doubt after
even a cursory examination of Mr. Lee's citations
and references. And indeed, the product itself,
as has been noticed, shows many of the ear-
marks of translation; it is stiff and splay,
dull, diffuse, and mechanical.

And yet in pirating, the Elizabethans did
modify the sonnet to some extent, slavish as
from Mr. Lee's account they may appear. As
every one knows nowadays, the Petrarchian
sonnet had a rhyming scheme in which not only
were the first eight lines, constituting the
octave, and the last six, the sestet, kept distinct, but also the two quatrains of the former
and the two tercets of the latter—a scheme to
which the phrasing itself was made to conform.
This was the discipline generally followed in
sixteenth-century Italy and was also adopted
by the French with an unimportant variation
of the sestet. In England, however, the inclination was to close with a couplet, whence it
became natural for the English to consider the
preceding twelve lines as made up of three sets
of fours and to rhyme then alternately, often
without any distinct or regular memberment,
as in Shakespeare's case.

As a result of this structural deformation there followed a change in the character, or at least in the effect, of the thought, due to the difference in the manner of developing it—a change, though important, to which Mr. Lee calls no particular attention. About the genuine sonnet there was a kind of parallelism encouraged by the two quatrains and the two tercets lying side by side, which imparted a peculiar movement to the ideas committed to their charge; and there was also a kind of cyclic or spiral progress initiated by the sestet, in accordance with which the sonnet, while rising, rounded again to its point of origin. Some allowance ought too to be made for the predominance of masculine rhymes over feminine; but such considerations would lead us too far afield. In the aggregate, then, notwithstanding the closeness with which the English repeated their masters, the change of construction, as it tended constantly to warp and disrupt the assemblage of parts, tended also to break up and modify the concatenation, and hence the general effect, of the ideas. And though it may be too much to say that in this way the English created a new *genre*, yet there can be no dcubt that they seriously transformed the old one—so much so that it can not be judged wholly by the same principles as the original.

Such is, in general, the natural history of the Elizabethan sonnet. In regard to some of

Mr. Lee's conclusions, however, a word or two
still remain to be said. Against the sonneteers
as a body he seems to have made out his case.
But to individual exceptions and occasional
felicities he is anything but sensitive. On their
literary side he has belittled the interest of the
sonnets, if not as a matter of principle, at least
consistently. To Lodge and Spenser, in particular, he shows but scant justice, to say nothing of
appreciation. A great robber Lodge may have
been, like Hawkins and Drake and Raleigh;
but at the same time there is a comparative
ease and fluency about his writing which may
explain, if not justify, the favourable opinion
traditionally held of him, upon which Mr. Lee
pounces with all the gleeful assurance of a positive method. Nor is it quite historical to con-
demn a man for the practices and manners
of his own age and society; while it ought to
be remembered that to convict an inhabitant
of those spacious times of looting, is not quite
the same thing as to convict him of literary
incompetence. As for Spenser, on the other
hand, Mr. Lee hardly gives him full credit for
the technical qualities of his *Amoretti*, though
he makes them a rather more liberal allowance
than is usual with him. The *Amoretti*, to be sure,
show no great inspiration; but they do show an
advanced knowledge of the musical capabilities
of verse, of which Mr. Lee says nothing.

Indeed, this mode of treatment is indicative of his whole procedure.   In his enthusiasm for his thesis he forgets that these men, for all their pilfering, preserve a distinctly personal flavour. In spite of conventionality and tradition a sonnet by Lodge is an entirely different matter from a sonnet by Daniel or Constable or any other of the poetic brotherhood.

> Thrice happy thou, Endymion, that embracest
> The livelong night thy love within thine arms.
> > Lodge: *Phillis*, xvii.

> Danger hath honour! great designs their fame!
> Glory doth follow!   Courage goes before!
> And though the event oft answers not the same;
> Suffice that high attempts have never shame.
> The Mean-Observer (whom base safety keeps)
> Lives without honour, dies without a name;
> And in eternal darkness ever sleeps.
> > Daniel: *Delia*, xxx.

> O that I never had been born at all!
> Or being, had been born of shepherds' brood!
> Then should I not in such mischances fall!
> Quiet my water;   and Content my food!
> > Barnes: *Parthenophil and Parthenope*, lxv.

> Anemone stood there with Daffodilly!
> The purple Hyacinth, and the musk Rose!
> Red Amaranthus, and the milk-bred Lily!
> > *Zepheria*, 33.

In other words, there is actually something in the work besides the model which it follows.

Even formally it is something more than a bare
transcript; for though the writers did not
succeed in making a correct sonnet, they did
occasionally succeed in making something which
is not a wholly unacceptable substitute.

> Not causeless were you christened, gentle flowers,
>   The one of faith, the other fancy's pride;
> For she who guides both faith and fancy's power,
>   In your fair colours laps her ivory side.
>
> .   .   .   .
>
> And as nor tyrant sun nor winter weather
>   May ever change sweet amaranthus hue,
> So she, though love and fortune join together,
>   Will never leave to be both fair and true.
>   Lodge: *Phillis*, xxviii.

And in modifying the movement and the character of the stanza in accordance with English
conditions they did also prepare a *genre* in
which Shakespeare was finally able to deliver
himself as he might not have been able to do
otherwise.

And surely this is no slight failing. To pass
judgment upon these sonneteers in the absence
of Shakespeare is very much like eliminating
its chief practitioner from a consideration of the
Elizabethan drama. What a sorry thing it
would be under those circumstances and how
false our notions of it! And yet Mr. Lee,
finding the sonnet without Shakespeare to be
nought, has turned about and applied this

conclusion to the belittlement of Shakespeare's. Nor is it altogether clear that he has fully perceived the intention of these sonneteers in themselves. The very possibility that all this work was actually meant in the main to be the very thing it is—an essay in ingenuity, an attempt to produce an "intellectual" poetry by a group of "wits," who were in a manner precursors of Donne and the "metaphysicals," and who would have resented the imputation of mere prettiness or even passion as bitterly as Cowley himself—such a possibility he seems to ignore altogether. And hence it is that, failing to relate it to life on the one hand, and on the other missing its most important literary affinity, he has failed, in so far, to grasp its vital significance as a poetic manifestation.

Will it seem unprofitably dilettanteish, then, if we add, in closing, that while a discussion of this kind is invaluable from one point of view, there is at the same time something rather dreary and unfilling about it, as there must always be in the discussion of matters purely formal? At all events it is certainly permissible to wish that so acute a scholar might have found time for some of the very significant ethical problems rising around his subject. What was there, for instance, in the disposition of the human spirit in the sixteenth century to give the sonnet such an immense vogue? What has

been the result of such a determination upon
our own social and individual culture? With
reference to the former question M. Doumic
has an interesting article in a recent number
of the *Revue des Deux Mondes*. In default of
any answer to the second it may be excusable,
for the sake of forming some idea of the relation
of all this literature to life, to risk ourselves
for a moment to a generalisation rather more
hazardous than a writer of Mr. Lee's reputation
for accuracy would probably care to undertake.

The young man who grows up into life
nowadays finds his behaviour and even his
emotional attitude toward the other sex
regulated for him largely in accordance with
certain generally understood traditions and
conventions. No matter how uncritical his
boyhood may have been, he now finds three sets
of feelings thoroughly, elaborately discriminated
—romantic love, marriage, and desire, and the
psychology, calculations, tactics, and so on
proper to each defined and codified. After
a little experience he himself is no longer in
danger of mixing matters; or if he should happen
to do so, he brings society with its average
common-sense about his ears. The distinction,
however, is obviously modern. The Greeks
knew nothing of it—at least systematically.
Euripides' Hecuba, in appealing to Agamemnon
to avenge the death of Polydorus, conjures

him by his love for Cassandra, whom she
speaks of as his wife but who is in reality his
concubine—a confusion intolerably shocking
to the present sense of propriety. And how
ambiguous to our minds is Helen's case! As
a matter of fact it is to the poets of the Renaissance and their later imitators and successors,
the French *Pléiade*, the Elizabethan sonneteers,
that we are indebted at least for the love part
of our code. Their conception of love is a sort
of humanistic blending of the Platonic admiration of abstract beauty with the mediæval
adoration of woman, and consists, therefore,
of two elements, answering in this fashion
to the constitution of the humanist himself—
a scholastic and a social ingredient.

To all these particular partitions—romantic
love, desire, and marriage—there is naturally
a common ground of passion patent or obscure.
Between imagination and passion the connection
is exceedingly close and compelling; and a vast
amount of poetry has been inspired by the
subterraneous promptings of this emotion, as
Mr. Santayana has justly indicated in his essay
on the *Sense of Beauty*. Such was undoubtedly
the original motive—or at least one of them—
behind the love poetry of the Renaissance. But
as the separation between love, marriage, and
desire was widened and confirmed by scholastic
and other influence then at work, passion was

restricted more and more to desire, while marriage became more subject to prudential calculation, and love itself to affectation until it gradually lost all its initiative and spontaneity. Virtually, therefore, the love sonnet, while preserving the convention, had by Shakespeare's time become sexless, and except for its personal pronouns might just as well be applied to men as to women. It is very significant, however, to notice that Shakespeare's sonnets do break through the convention; he is singular in admitting passion into the love sonnet and confounding the categories—a fact that would lead one to infer that Mr. Lee has in his life exaggerated the element of artificiality and imitation in Shakespeare's work. But however this may be, it is evident that the modern feeling for women is changing so rapidly as to be no longer represented by this old literature, the appreciation of which is obviously waning, though we still employ something of the old form and circumstance and shall continue to do so until we can beat out a new ethics—that is, in all probability for some little time to come.

BALZAC

THERE are few writers so difficult to range and pronounce upon, even before the informal tribunal of one's own consciousness, as Honoré Balzac—or de Balzac, as he loved with childish vanity to hear himself called. [1] His ill-assorted literary gifts—huddled together as promiscuously as the various litter of the old curiosity shop in the *Peau de Chagrin*—the dulness of his spiritual perceptions, his total insensibility to many of the nobler aspects of life, his coarseness, sensationalism, and brutality —these in connection with his inexhaustible fecundity, the fervour of his imagination, and his riotous creativeness make up a bewildering and disconcerting personality. With the possible exception of a few short stories there is hardly a piece, certainly not a book, in the whole collection which is a thoroughly creditable performance, even in point of workmanship. Nor at the same time is there a single piece which does not somewhere convey an impression of tremendous though convulsive power, as if

[1] The Temple Edition of the *Comédie Humaine*. Edited by George Saintsbury. New York: The Macmillan Co.

it had been forged cold in some terrible paroxysm of genius. But whatever one's literary prepossessions, there is the man, forty volumes of him, an undeniable influence, which must be reckoned with some way or other.

Personally he would seem to have been one of those ardent and energetic natures, the modern *bedeutendes individuum* or "strong" man, unsoftened by more than the slightest trace of sentiment and possessed by a rage of work so furious as to be all but unconscious of the doubts and hesitations of finer temperaments. His one passion is power; his notion of the world, a struggle, where victory is won by strength, courage, and audacity. To him success is in no way a matter of morals; the battle is to the brave, not to the righteous. It is this practical view of life which makes him seem so one-sided and deficient, not to say objectionable, to those who think that fiction exists, regardless of truth, for the vindication of the moral order. For himself he saw in literature his way to the exercise of the power which he loved with the violence of his kind. His whole character in its assumption and ambition is epitomised in the line which he inscribed below his bust of Napoleon: "What he could not achieve with his sword, I will accomplish with my pen."

His life, as it has been passed on to us, reads like the wildest romance of authorship, riddled with preposterous debts, undermined by conspiracies, centred about with fabulous intrigues —so falsified, in short, by the forgeries of his imagination, in which his friends unduly encouraged him, that it is no longer possible to disentangle truth from—well, let us say, with Goethe, poetry. For, at worst, he was hardly more than his own dupe, confounding reality with illusion to such an extent that he seemed to see the characters of his own fiction visibly walking in the streets of Paris, and supposed his rooms to be sumptuously furnished when he had scrawled upon the bare walls in chalk the names of the luxuries which he coveted. But amid all these extravagances of an overwrought fancy the one fact is certain. Abandoned by his family to the pursuit of letters, without means or genuine literary gifts, unless the desire for literary fame be such in itself, he fought his way to success, in the very teeth of starvation and, as it were, against the express prohibition of nature, by sheer dint of perseverance and capacity for labour. His was perhaps the longest and severest apprenticeship ever served by a great writer; his unacknowledged work alone would constitute in quantity a very respectable achievement. And yet he never succeeded in mastering a style or acquiring a form. To the last his work is confused and amorphous, crammed with all sorts of irrelevant details, crowded with episodes, and distracted by pretentious rigmarole anent the nearest trifle, the placing of a patch on a woman's face, or the relative merit of round waists and flat. At most he learned how to wreak his strength upon his readers, browbeating and domineering over them until at last they succumb to the imposition of that despotic personality.

Such a man can never make "agreeable" reading, when every literary defect is faced with a moral lack. And yet upon some minds—and they are neither few nor commonplace—he acts like a powerful stimulant. That the fascination is generally uncanny and frequently morbid may be allowed; but that it is on the whole genuine is proved by the fact that he has long survived Eugene Sue, into whose province and that of the police court the remoter confines of his realm, as the whole Vautrin cycle, shade imperceptibly. For these minds, it is the man's ineradicable romance, or, to grant the most at once to his detractors, his sensationalism, which constitutes his perennial charm. For after all, his naturalism, of which so much has been made, as there are always those who insist upon admiring an author for the wrong thing, is only superficial. His circumstantial descriptions, his parade of affairs, his "physiology," are all but pretences, the cloak that he assumes to disguise the enormity of his fabrications. At bottom he is a dexterous manipulator of intrigues, a manager of "powerful" situations, and a maker of high sententious phrases. It is for the sake of his bewitching duchesses with their melodiously nasal "*Hein*," who bear the burden of their thirty years so jauntily, his outrageous scamps like Maxime de Trailles, his whole gallery of preposterous and admirable prodigies, the Marneffes, the Rastignacs, the Goriots, that we delight in him.

But there is another side to his genius—to us, we frankly confess, by no means so interesting as the former because less characteristic and more commonplace. In the delineation of virtue it cannot be denied that Balzac is surpassed by many an inferior talent. And while *Eugenie Grandet* is very likely, on the whole, one of his best books, the character of old Grandet being strictly in his own best vein, yet in general innocence and delicacy suffer sad distortion at his violent hands, and probably no more grotesque book was ever written nor one in worse taste than *Le Lys dans la Vallée*, to which he sat down with the avowed intention of drawing an exemplary portrait.

It was in 1836, according to his own story, that the notion of the *Comédie Humaine* took shape in his mind, though it was not until six years later that he found himself at the head

of a production large enough to justify the
announcement of a conception so stupendous.
His idea was nothing less than that of correlating
all his work, past and future, into one vast
system having for its end the complete depiction
of French society in all its phases and activities
—its businesses, professions, philosophy, science,
art, government, religion, in all its nooks and
crannies, country, province, and city—in fact,
in all its multifarious, pullulating life.

Behind this design there is, as might be
surmised, a pretence of cosmical philosophy,
partly sincere and partly, it may be suspected,
in the nature of one of those gigantic hoaxes
of which Balzac was so fond, and by which
he himself was usually the first to be duped.
Avowedly his point of departure is Geoffroy
Saint-Hilaire's well-known postulate, that the
differentiation of animals is brought about
entirely by the individual's adaptation to its
environment.   Following this clue, Balzac
came to see in humanity a different species
for every pursuit.   And as the natural historian
could make up his account of the animal only
as a function of its environment, he aspired
in the same way to become the natural historian
of society—a task which was complicated
over that of his scientific colleague by the
presence in society of three sets of disturbing factors totally absent from the animal

kingdom: woman, who is more than female to the man; intelligence, which confuses the struggle for existence; and possessions, which, by influencing men's habits, dress, and speech, increase the natural divergencies distractingly.

It is always necessary to follow a writer with some caution when he begins to theorise about his own work. At the same time it is interesting to notice here the intrusion into letters of that kind of scientific pretension which was to continue to our own day and figure so largely with Zola and his Experimental Novel. And though we may suspect that Balzac, like his modern admirer, had read too many scientific books which he could not understand, this after all is his most original contribution to the idea of the novel. Writing before the formulation of evolution, he was the first in letters to grasp the general principle that man is generally what his circumstances make him, and, acting courageously on this conviction, the first to rescue him from the half-abstract being he was rapidly becoming in fiction, by reintegrating him in his *milieu*. And so, if Rousseau was the first, as Sainte-Beuve says, to introduce verdure, Balzac may be said, with an accent of, praise or blame as one looks at these things, to have been the first to introduce money, into literature.

But let us not be carried too far. Solemnly

as he took himself, let us beware of becoming
his dupes ourselves. In spite of his pretensions
to scientific method, he is little less than ridiculous as a serious thinker. Not only is his reasoning confused and obscure, it is naturally
erratic and unbalanced. He appears to have
had one of those heads which embroil whatever
is thrown into them. To all appearance an idea
recommended itself to him not because it was
reasonable or even specious, but because it was
strange, outlandish, unexpected, amazing. It
was the impossible that he preferred to believe.
He regrets that modern education makes no
provision for the study of the "occult sciences."
On one occasion he is said to have written to Dr.
Chapelain, inquiring why the physicians had
not made use of somnambulists to discover the
cause of cholera. For his own part he frequently consulted somnambulists about the health
of friends at a distance—and fortune-tellers
about his future. However vivid his portraits
and vignettes, he had no consistent philosophy
of life to impart—or aught that we can not
neglect, if we like, with perfect safety. At most
his work has a mechanical congruity; it seems
to coincide with certain of the more persistent
data of experience. It is preoccupied with
money and business; and money and business,
as everybody knows, constitute the one serious
and constant reality. But in that case the con-

clusion appears inevitable; the novel should
be turned over to the economists and sociolo-
gists. And willingly for my part would I
surrender to the curious student of "social conditions" the whole "documentary" Balzac, of
whom so much has been already written, provided only I might be allowed to keep the
extravagant and caricaturist. Whether he
intended it or not, he is almost the only Frenchman who is a humourist in something the same
sense as Dickens. There is about him a broad-
ness, an excess, a robustiousness—in short, an
exhilarating violation of the just measure,
which distinguishes him from his own countrymen. He is not a wit, nor does he write
comedy in the French acceptation,—but something quite different, something bigger and more
obstreperous and nearer Ben Jonson. His

" *Vous n' êtez pas assez fort pour la vie de
Paris* ";

"Madame, you have touched that axe";
his

"Sir, would you kill a man for my sake?"
"Two, Madame";

his Rastignac bidding Paris defiance across old
Goriot's grave—these things have just the delightful incommunicable thrill so rare in French. Such
quality may possibly destroy Balzac's authority
for the native reader; it has proved a stumbling-
block to the critics; it is responsible, as much

as anything, for the confusion that exists with regard to his "significance." But nevertheless it is this, I venture to think, which makes his great attraction for the English reader. And this, it should be noticed, is not fact, it is not transcription, or imitation, or "document," or anything of the kind; it is imagination or transmutation—or, in a word, creation.

And indeed such as he was, and we have seen that he was by no means faultless, he remains in his own way one of the very few geniuses who, like Shakespeare, are in any just sense creators. For the *Comédie Humaine* is more or less, as you please, than literature; it is a kind of life itself, a world of good and evil, with the evil in disheartening excess, perhaps, but the likest of man's creation, in that as in other respects, to the world in which we live. It is incoherent, confused, and fragmentary; often dull, frequently trivial, always unsettling, but altogether incalculable and amazing, the very spectacle of human life. And yet, fragmentary as it is, for he never brought his project to completion, a monstrous Babel, as Zola calls it, with its forty volumes and its two thousand characters appearing and disappearing and reappearing like the faces in the street, it still looms colossal in its ruins, "*puissant et solitaire*" as the monuments of a vanished civilisation, testifying to the gigantic powers of its architect.

GEORGE SAND

THOUGH it is probably true that the influence once exerted by George Sand upon the youth of England, as commemorated in Matthew Arnold's appreciation of that remarkable woman, was as a matter of fact only temporary and exceptional, yet there was a certain justice and reason in it, while it lasted, not always discernible in literary enthusiasms. Little as George Sand was of the English way of thinking in other respects, she did, perhaps more than any other great French novelist, conceive of literary composition in the English way. It has always been more or less characteristic of the English that they should value writing for its spontaneity, for its natural and unexpected graces, rather than for perfection of workmanship and finish. To the Englishman writing is a gift, not an art, and he has never been tempted to confound the two. This is the reason that style and construction have counted for so relatively little in the English novel, that even so great a novelist as Thackeray has no composition to speak of, and that a person with so vicious a manner as George Meredith's should have received so high a rating as a writer.

And yet at its best, Mr. Meredith does not,
as a matter of fact, suit much better with the
English ideal than he does with the French, for
the former does imply, for all its lapses, a
preference at least for the natural.

The fact is, the English have formed their
written upon the model of their spoken style.
They seem, as it were, to assume that their
literature is written offhand, and must be
judged, even a little indulged, it may be, with this
circumstance in mind; as though it were to be
expected of an author, not that he should necessarily give long time and thought to his expression, but that he should write quickly
and fluently, above all naturally—in short,
as though his best possession were the pen of the
ready writer. What he has accomplished, then,
is to be criticised in accordance with these
conditions, not as aiming at perfection, at the
expense of unlimited pains and patience, at
any cost! On the contrary, the main require-
ment made of himself by the French writer
is that he attain this perfection, which the
former has left as unattainable or inconvenient
or impertinent—a perfection absolute and
final, which he has always before his eyes as the
goal of his aspirations and towards which he
strives relentlessly. Time and labour are no
object; only that when the work leaves his
pen-cramped hand it shall be the best that can

be made out of words, the very best without reserve or abatement. Ease, or at least the appearance of ease, may be desirable; not, however, because it is the main purpose of writing to write easily, but because it is a property of elegance that whatever is done, no matter with what difficulty, should be done too well to show the effort. But diffuseness, approximation, confusion, and the like unavoidable accompaniments of conversationalism and improvisation are forever unpardonable equally with the appearance of stress and strain. While the English write prose with something of the carelessness of talk, the French write prose with the same care that we give to poetry.

It is impossible to describe this state of mind better than Maupassant has done in speaking of an author who stands in every respect in the most striking contrast with George Sand, and who represents most characteristically the literary tendencies and ideals, if not the actual performance, of his countrymen—Gustave Flaubert.

Haunted by this absolute belief that there exists but one way of expressing a thing, one word to name it, one adjective to qualify it, one verb to animate it, he [Flaubert] would devote himself to superhuman efforts to discover for every phrase that word, that epithet, that verb. In this way he believed in a mysterious harmony of expressions, and when a word otherwise suitable seemed to him to lack euphony, he would go on searching for another with invincible patience, sure that he had not yet found the true, the unique word.

For him writing was a redoubtable undertaking, full of torment, peril, and weariness.   He would seat himself at his table in fear and love of that dear distracting business.   .   .   .

Then he would begin to write slowly, stopping again and again, beginning over and over, erasing, interlining, filling the margins, criss-crossing, spoiling twenty pages for one he finished, and groaning with the effort of thought like a wood-sawyer.

Sometimes, tossing his pen into a great oriental pewter tray which he kept full of carefully cut goose-quills, he would seize his sheet of paper, raise it to the level of his eyes, and, leaning on his elbow, begin to declaim in a loud, rasping voice, listening the while to the rhythm of his prose, pausing to catch a fugitive reverberation, combining the tones, separating the assonances, and disposing commas cunningly like resting-places on a long road.

.   .   .   .

A thousand preoccupations would beset him at once, but this desperate certainty always remained fixed in his mind: "Among all these phrases, forms, and turns of expression there is but one phrase, one form, one turn of expression to represent what I want to say."

And, red in the face, with swollen cheeks and neck, his muscles tense like a straining athlete's, he would struggle frantically with idea and expression, coupling them in spite of themselves, holding them indissolubly together by the force of his will, grasping the thought and subjugating it little by little with superhuman effort and fatigue, and caging it up, like a captive beast, in a solid and exact form.

How excessive, but at the same time how indicative in its excess of the writer's scrupulousness. Nor is it only Flaubert; it is La Bruyère also who speaks to the same effect in almost identically the same words.

Among all the different expressions by which a single one of our thoughts may be rendered, there is only one which is right, though we do not always hit upon it in speaking or writing. It is true, however, that it exists; and everything else is feeble and unsatisfactory to a man of intelligence who wishes to be understood.

And while the passion for perfection may not be quite so virulent with every one of their countrymen as it was with these two, yet was there ever an Englishman, however exceptional, who conceived of writing quite like this? It is necessary only to compare these remarks with our traditions of Scott's indefatigable pen and Shakespeare's unblotted lines in order to recognise how different the spirit of French and English prose.

This difference of style as between the two nations may be referred, at least in effect, to a variety of causes, the most influential of which are probably these three.

In the first place the Englishman has never made so wide a divorce between thinking and writing as has the Frenchman. The former has temperamentally given thought such a decided pre-eminence over the presentation of thought

3

that he has hardly considered the two as separate at all; but when he has had anything to write, has been content simply to think it out in words, and let it go at that. He has always managed to say what he wanted to say, if he has talked long enough; and writing is a sort of soliloquy in which no one can interrupt him. Consider how Browning conducts a poem, like a monologue upon which his readers are licensed for the nonce to eavesdrop, quite welcome to whatever, if anything, they can manage to pick up. One can, to be sure, put down his book, or throw it away; but his attitude under such circumstances is one of haughty indifference—he writes no better. The Frenchman, on the contrary, while thinking, considers that he is in privacy and may be as informal as he likes. In expressing himself, however, he remembers that he is in the presence of others, whom he is eager to please and impress—he feels that he must strike and maintain his pose.

> To write a letter [says Renan] is a torture to me. I can understand how one man makes a display of skill before ten as well as before ten thousand; but before a single person! Before writing I hesitate, I reflect, I make a plan for a scrawl of four pages.

In short, to the Frenchman writing is a social art, an affair of manners. As Brunetière says in words almost identical with Goethe's:

From Crestien de Troyes . . . to M. François Coppée
. . . hardly any one in France has written otherwise than in view of society and without ever separating
the expression of his thought from a regard for the
public to whom he has addressed himself, and as a
result the art of writing from that of pleasing, per-
suading, convincing.

Or in other words thought is one thing, presentation quite another. And when the Frenchman
comes to write, it is the result rather than the
process that he aims to give, and then crystal-
lised in polished sentences which shall have
something of the finality of a formula, and fore-
stall posterity. When he has once said a
thing it is said forever. From this peculiarity
of his mind results the importance taken in his
literature by epigram.

Beside this intellectual difference between
the two nations there exists also a difference
of language which, though it may be sprung
from the former, must be spoken of separately.
French words, partly through the influence of the
Academy, have comparatively little of that
indistinctness or blur of outline, that sort of
emotional penumbra which is so noticeable with
English words and to which English poetry
owes in great part its haunting suggestiveness.
On the contrary, they are defined and outlined,
stamped clean to the very edges, covering the
ideas upon which they are set with a nicety and
exactitude that make French, for all its narrow

vocabulary, an ideal instrument of thought. About most English words there is something vague, floating, elusive—something left over to be accounted for after they are applied to the ideas which they symbolise. And this fringe of meaning, which scatters such an iridescent halo about English poetry, makes it necessary in English prose, where such diffraction is an embarrassment, to qualify, limit, and extenuate in order to define the thought with accuracy.

But these two conditions, far as they go, are not enough in themselves to explain all the phenomena we have been observing and have still to observe. It is necessary to take account also of a total difference as between the conceptions of genius held by the two peoples. Genius to the Frenchman means essentially an infinite capacity for taking pains—an intelligence capable of discerning the nature of the end proposed, of holding it steadily in view, and of applying cunningly and patiently every means at hand to its attainment. Characteristically, the ends of French genius are always rational, attainable by the eminently reasonable man—the man, it may almost be said, of common ideas and uncommon energies. To every race genius is the apotheosis it makes of its own best faculty; and intelligence is the Frenchman's best faculty, as imagination is the Englishman's.

"Our literature," declares Nisard in his well-known characterisation of the French spirit, "is, as it were, the living image of this government of the faculties by reason. . . . This is the spectacle offered us by our masterpieces—they display nothing but a higher reason, sufficiently reinforced by the love of truth to dominate the imagination and the senses and to draw admirable assistance whence ordinarily come the greatest dangers." From this eminently practical point of view there is nothing absurd in Flaubert's sitting down with the avowed intention of producing a classic—and succeeding in doing so. While by the very fact his opinion concerning the spirit of the literature, which he knew well enough to produce a masterpiece in it by malice prepense, takes on a representative character.

Talent, he declares for his part, and to appreciate the force of the word the reader must remember that it is one maker of *chefs-d'œuvre* coaching another,[1] Talent is only long patience. Everything which one desires to express must be looked at with sufficient attention and during a sufficiently long time to discover in it some aspect which no one has as yet seen or described. In everything there is still some spot unexplored. . . . The smallest object contains something unknown. Find it. To describe a fire that flames, and a tree on a plain, look, keep looking, at that flame and that tree

[1] Introduction to Maupassant's *Pierre et Jean*, trans. by Hugh Craig.

till in your eyes they have lost all resemblance to any
other tree or any other fire.

This is the way to become original.

To the Englishman, on the contrary, genius
signifies something more, at least something
other than the free play of intelligence. It
implies inspiration, as he calls it—the revelation
that seems to come down like a sudden light
upon life, laying bare its very secrets, trans-
muting it with new meaning, and possessing
the writer, like one beside himself, with an
enthusiasm, a power, an eloquence beyond
his own. "Poetry," declares Hazlitt, as though
in direct contradiction of Nisard, "signifies the
excess of the imagination beyond the actual or
ordinary impression of an object or feeling. The
poetical impression of any object is that uneasy,
exquisite sense of beauty or power that can not
be contained within itself, that is impatient
of all limit." And for this capricious, heady,
lawless spirit, this emotional transport and exaltation, this genius which ravishes and immor-
talises its possessor, it is doubtful whether the
Frenchman has ever in reality acquired a thoroughly unqualified admiration, in spite of his
theatrical raptures over *le grand Williams*—any
more so, indeed, than the Englishman has succeeded in appreciating the pale, refrigerated
splendour of Racine. "We are very much mistaken," cries Zola, "when we think that the

characteristic of a good style is a sublime confusion with just a dash of madness in it; in reality the merit of a style depends upon its logic and clearness." The Frenchman, in a word, tends always to subjectivise his emotion and possses it, thereby making his literature objective; while the Englishman tends to objectivise his and to allow it to possess him, thereby making his literature subjective.

Agreeable with this distinction is Heine's division of writers into two classes: those who cultivate "an orderly arrangement, an editing, so to speak, of the thought, a logical composition of the parts of speech—in brief, the architecture of the period"; and those who, "when they would write well, must work themselves up into a state of passionate excitement, a kind of mental intoxication—Bacchants of thought who stumble after the god in sacred inebriety." And it is just this difference, whether it has its roots in character or cultivation, which is critically differential of French and English—the difference, in other words, between art and genius. Language is at best an inadequate medium, no matter how well handled. And one in accordance with his temperament will prefer the relatively imperfect embodiment of a lofty ideal; and another, the well-rounded embodiment of a relatively low ideal. The former produces a literature

of aspiration, in which the whole structure of
language is bent and strained by the stress of
meaning forced upon it, a romantic literature
strong in poetry and weak in prose, like English.
The latter produces a finished and finite literature, neat, elegant, and limited, strong in prose
and weak in poetry, a literature of ideas, a classic
literature, like French.   For the exuberance
of life always tends to shatter and demolish
form; and it is only by painful labour, by clip-
ping and paring and pruning, that a fresh and
modern existence can be forced into vessels
and moulds.   This is probably something of
what Flaubert meant by his celebrated and oft-
quoted remark, "The idea springs from the
form," a saying so hard for the Englishman,
and yet almost a shibboleth to his own disciples.
At all events the remark has this much truth:
in Goethe's words, "*die Kunst ist nur Gestaltung*,"
art is only form; and in determining his form,
in finding what he can or can not put into
language without rupturing it, the artist does at
least determine what his idea shall be.   To this
general effect George Sand writes to Flaubert:
"It seems to me that your school does n't
pay enough attention to the inwardness of things
and is too much inclined to rest satisfied with
their superficies.   As a consequence of searching
for form you neglect the profundities and
address yourself only to the literati."   Ay;

but he knew that he could not render the profundities without doing violence to the shape and figure of his work, and that he would not do. As Mr. Henry James says, "He had no faith in the power of the moral to offer a surface."

For these causes, principal among others, English literature is distinguished from French by its preference, at least in effect, for improvisation and inspiration. And it is for this reason, because these are so exactly the characteristics of her writing, that George Sand deserves the attention of the English reader. "No writer," asserts Mr. James, "has produced such great effects with an equal absence of premeditation." Her spontaneity, ease, and fluency, her individuality, sensibility, and inventiveness are the positive virtues which most please the English sense; while the vices of their reverse—her diffuseness, confusion, and haziness, her irregularity, extravagance, and wilfulness, in fine her lack of discipline—are all defects which the English least notice or most readily excuse. She had no art in the strict sense; but she had inspiration, its virtues and vices, its qualities and defects.

The essential truth of this judgment of George Sand has never been disputed by her countrymen or indeed by herself. "She knows," writes Balzac, "and said of herself just what I think, without saying it to her, namely, that she has neither force of conception, nor gift of constructing plots, nor faculty of reaching the true, nor the art of pathos, but—without knowing the French language—she has *style;* and that is true." But in spite of the charm of her writing, almost irresistible in the wooing of the soft slow sentences, the inevitable weaknesses of the facility which stood her in place of literary method have been observed over and over, particularly where they are most noticeable, in her construction. Her lack of fundamental plan, of architectural design, has impaired a work that otherwise would have in perfection, as it now has in bulk, few peers. Sentences she could write, and chapters, exquisite in touch and feeling,—few better; but alas! for all their delicacy, fragments. When it comes to building up piece by piece a single whole, an entire fabric with the subdual of many parts to the perfect harmony of one great purpose,—there her weakness, the weakness of facility, is manifest. "*Le génie,*" she says herself, "*vient du cœur et ne réside pas dans la forme";* and it was her misfortune to take her own statement too literally—so literally, indeed, that in Flaubert's sense she had no form at all.

For to Flaubert, as Maupassant observes, form meant something more comprehensive than style.

While attaching great importance to observation and

analysis, he attached an even greater importance to composition and style. In his opinion it was these two qualities in especial which made a book imperishable. By composition he understood that obstinate labor which consists in expressing only the essence of the successive acts of a life, in choosing only the characteristic traits, and in grouping and combining them so that they shall concur perfectly to the effect intended.

It was not merely his language, then, for which Flaubert was so anxiously concerned in his obstinate wrestlings with expression—it was as well the figure, the shape, the whole concrete plastic embodiment— the *Gestaltung*—under which he should exhibit his conception, at once the emanation and the incorporation of the idea as surely as the pose of a statue is decisive of the final impression produced, to which the style was to add its particular evocation of sentiment like the music of an opera. This was his conception of form, a complete organic whole, a creation in all its parts fatally answerable to the thought of its creator. In the words of Stevenson, who suffered under much the same obsession of literary conscience as Flaubert:

For the welter of impression, all forcible but all discreet, which life presents, it [art] substitutes a certain artificial series of impressions, all indeed most feebly represented, but all aiming at the same effect, all eloquent of the same idea, all chiming together like consonant notes in music or like the graduated tints in a good picture. From all its chapters, from all its pages,

from all its sentences, the well-written novel echoes and
re-echoes its one creative and controlling thought; to
this must every incident and character contribute; the
style must have been pitched in unison with this;
and if there is anywhere a word that looks another way,
the book would be stronger, clearer, and (I had almost
said) fuller without it. Life is monstrous, infinite,
illogical, abrupt, and poignant; a work of art in comparison is neat, finite, self-contained, rational, flowing,
and emasculate.

It is hardly surprising that of form in this
consummate interpretation, as the deliberate
artist understands it, George Sand should show
small sense. With her quick, sensitive, and
rather shallow nature she was by no means so
likely to distinguish herself through the manifestation of intellect and will in literature as
through the manifestation of sentiment and
emotion—not so much in composition as in
style. For these, as nearly as they can be
discriminated, would seem to be the particular
powers of the two. On the whole it is upon the
writer's manner, his choice of words and his way
of assorting them, that the emotional tone or
colour of his work depends. It is by his style
or not at all that he succeeds in imparting
a personal warmth and glow to his writing.
Nothing is more curious at first sight than the
manner in which certain literary tendencies
become associated with certain articles of
dress—the blue coat and buff waistcoat of the

Wertherites, the Byronic collar, the scarlet
waistcoat of romanticism, the pre-Raphaelites'
velvet jacket, Walt Whitman's broad hat and
blue flannel shirt. And in just the same way it
is easily intelligible how a disposition or a temperament should express itself in its use of
language; while the intellectual, the mental
constitution is manifested rather in the relation
and connection of ideas, the combination of
parts, the composition of the several members,
the structure or synthesis of the writing as a
whole. A Greek tragedy imposed, not by its
emotional and sentimental surface play, but
by its deep purposefulness, its severe determin-
ism; and so to a lesser degree the drama of
Racine, and to some extent all genuinely
characteristic French work as compared with
English; while a poem of Shelley's or Tennyson's,
on the contrary, pleases by the prismatic shim-
mer of sentiment with which it is overlaid. The
one is typically the affair of composition, the
other of style. And toward the latter extreme
George Sand's writing naturally gravitates
in spite of the general tradition to which it
belongs. It is full of colour and feeling, it is
splendidly romantic; but when one comes to
consider it as a whole, to look toward its end
and reflect upon its tendency, one is struck
by its ineptitude to its purpose.

In this respect her work corresponds very

closely with the account she herself gives of her own intellectual condition: "Wisdom," she remarks very justly, "consists perhaps in classifying one's impressions, in keeping them from encroaching upon one another, and in isolating, if necessary, the particular impression one wishes to receive. In this way arise the great works of genius." And of herself:

> In order to put an end to my lack of mental discipline I have prescribed myself a regular life and a daily task —and then two-thirds of the time I lose myself in dreaming or reading or writing something very different from that in which I ought to be absorbed. Had it not been for this intellectual dissipation I should have acquired some sort of an education, for I comprehend readily enough—indeed, if anything, I get to the bottom of things a little too readily; I should have forced my memory to classify its ideas. To understand and to know has been my constant aspiration; but of what I have wished to realise I have realised nothing. My will has never governed my thought. . . . The external has always acted upon me more than I have acted upon it. I have become a mirror from which my own image is obliterated, so completely is it filled with a confused reflection of figures and objects.

These characteristic mental traits of hers show themselves in her writing in several ways. For the careful and consistent reader one of the most painful experiences is prepared by the frequency with which she falls away in the latter part of her novels from the high standard of her beginnings,—and that not merely in her early work, when she was learning her trade, but in the work of after periods as well, when she had served a long apprenticeship to her art. It is sad to notice, for instance, that M. Faguet speaks of the first volume of a story like the *Beaux Messieurs de Bois Doré* as a *chef-d'œuvre* and then drops the remainder of it into the oblivion of silence as though in mercy of its defects. And it is sadder still to find for oneself a book of such fair promise, which might have been completed faultlessly within the limit of three hundred pages, running on into a wreck of diminishing climaxes and crises and feeble after-thoughts, until it expires tardily of sheer exhaustion, without the needed apology for being so long a-dying, at more than twice its natural age,—spoiled for no other apparent reason than that the writer wrote too easily to stop when she had finished. Of her might be said what Dryden says of Fletcher: "He is a true Englishman—he knows not when to give over." It is hardly exaggeration to advise one wishing to read George Sand's best work to read only the first halves of her novels.

And yet the difficulty were not to be so escaped. This fault of saying too much, this plethora of words occurs again and again over smaller areas than an entire book. With the inveteracy of disease it infects the whole system. The author is not willing to make the

reader a suggestion, to drop him a hint, to
risk herself to his perspicacity. She must needs
explain—often more for her own sake than for
his, it would appear—until there is left over
event and motive hardly a single shadow for him
to penetrate, but everything lies exposed in an
even glare of revelation, like the monotonous
landscape of our great western prairie, without
concealment or mystery. There are no skeletons
in George Sand's closet; she has got them all
out into the middle of the floor.   And her
dialogue is as prolix as her analysis.   Her
characters seem possessed with her own fondness
for explication, and invariably talk matters out
to a finish, however trivial, so that the reader
is constantly outrunning the writer with a sense
at the end of disillusion and disappointment.
This circumstance is partly accountable for the
feeling of commonplaceness which frequently
torments one in his George Sand, even in what
he is conscious on reflection are the rarest
aperçus. The development of her thought
is so slow, so gradual, so far foreseen that her
utterances are stamped with none of that
surprise which we have come to consider as the
hallmark of a profound saying. One is so long
prepared that, when the announcement finally
comes, it falls flat on his tired ear like an assertion of the obvious.

Perhaps this faultiness, behind which lies

always her too ready fluency, may be explained,
or at least illustrated, by her manner of work.
It is well known nowadays, when the personal
habits of authors are more studied than their
books, that she wrote at night for certain fixed
hours with the regularity of a day-labourer.
" She works every night," so Goncourt reports,
" from one to four, and then sets to work again
during the day for a couple of hours—and . . .
it makes no difference if she's disturbed. . . .
Imagine that you have a faucet open in the
house; some one comes in, you close it. . . .
That's the way with Mme. Sand." The story
goes of her that if she happened to finish the
novel on which she was employed an hour or
even less before her time was up for the night,
she would calmly set the manuscript away, the
ink still damp on the page, and placidly begin
another, composing rapidly as she went until
the clock released her. Whether rightly or
wrongly one misses something here—the fond
lingering over the old work, the patient review
and minute revision, the reluctance to part with
the child of the brain which makes every *finis* to
the author a lover's parting and which is so
characteristic of the French writers of the
century.

It is another story that Maupassant tells
of Flaubert:

When he read to his friends the tale entitled, *Un*

4

Cœur simple, several remarks and criticisms were passed
on a passage of ten lines, in which the old maid ends
by confounding her parrot with the Holy Ghost.   The
idea seemed too subtle for the mind of a peasant.
Flaubert listened, reflected, recognised the justice
of the observation—but was seized with agony.
"You're right," he said," only—I should have to
alter my phrase."

That very evening, however, he set to work.   He
spent the night in changing ten words; he blackened
and cancelled twenty sheets of paper, and finally left
things as they were, unable to construct another
phrase whose harmony would satisfy him.

In the beginning of the same tale the final word of
a paragraph serving as the subject of the following,
might give rise to an amphibology.   This distraction
was pointed out to him; he recognised it and attempted
to change the sense, but could not recover the sonority
which he wished for, and, discouraged, exclaimed;
"So much the worse for the sense; rhythm before
everything !!"

Can there be a more significant contrast than
that between these two pictures: Flaubert, the
great, rough, positive Norman, hesitating ir-
resolutely over a novel for seven years, unable
either to perfect or relinquish it; and George
Sand, the woman, feeble and timorous, one
might suppose, resolutely laying aside one
piece of work and taking up another in order
to fill out half an hour of scheduled time?   By
comparison there is something very like grandeur
—the grandeur of renunciation, perhaps—
in this ability of hers to put away the past

when she was done with it, to leave her work
to its deserts without just one more backward
look, just one more correction, and to pass on
confidently to the next duty without worrying
over what was gone.

> *Consuelo*, she writes in reply to a letter of Flaubert's,
> *la Comtesse de Rudolstadt*, what in the world is that?
> Can it be something of mine?   I have forgotten every
> last treacherous word of it.   Do you read it?   Does
> it really amuse you?   In that case I will re-read it
> one of these days and if you like me I shall like myself.

Such a remark is possible only to a large and
spacious spirit.

> It often seems, said Goethe on one occasion to Ecker-
> mann, as though my own things were altogether
> foreign to me.   To-day I happened to be reading some-
> thing in French, and as I read, I thought—the man
> speaks quite cleverly, I should n't say it otherwise
> myself.   And when I looked more closely, I saw it was
> a piece of my own translated.

At all events it shows a self-detachment, a
sobriety and moderation which is often sadly
to seek in French literary workmanship of the
modern school, with its long brooding, its
slow coagulation, its overlaid and half-addled
conception, such as we have come to connect
even with Balzac, who would never let his
copy go, so Gautier tells us, till it was wrung
from him by his implacable taskmaster, the
publisher.

But for all this excess of care we might well wish that George Sand had, without going too far, shown a little more concern for what she had done, a little more for what she was about to do, were it reasonable to suppose that all her errors were due to her habits of work and could have been retrieved by revision. Much, however, of her defective construction must be charged to another cause. A certain indefiniteness of conception, a failure to decide the end from the beginning and write up to it—in short, a powerlessness to fix and realise the idea of a book, is equally a condition of her structural frailty. "Descriptions and paintings," Brunetière insists, "are no proof that one knows how to write; they prove only that one has strong sensations. What is expected of the writer is the expression of general ideas, and by that he is judged." For after all our talk about concreteness and what not, does not every great novel rest finally upon an idea, which the story serves as a specific instance to illustrate? It is difficult perhaps to determine but it is surely legitimate to ask whether the masters have not invariably seen in their fables something wider than the single incident recorded, something standing to that incident in the relation of a general principle to a particular case. In Brunetière's words again: "It is not enough to have seen, to have observed; it is essential

besides that something general in the case of
science, something universally human in the
case of art, should be, as it were, engaged in our
very observation." Certain it is, at all events
that we can not think of a novel in any sense
great which does not result for us in some conclusion, much more comprehensive than the
case in point, in regard to human life and conduct. It may not be expressible in other terms
than those particular ones in which the author
has rendered it; it may not lend itself to
intellectual formularisation at all; but there it
is in the reader's mind as the residuum of his
reading—the book simple, concrete, and special;
the idea complex, abstract, and universal.
And it is hardly reasonable to suppose that the
writer could have got it thither unless he wrote
with it constantly before his eyes. So true
is this that the idea a book leaves with us
becomes its criterion. "When such a philosophical theme," so Taine insists, "meets a person
capable of carrying it to the end and expressing
it completely, the novel is of the first order,"
while Lessing makes a similar distinction from
the complementary point of view:

To create for a purpose, to imitate for a purpose,
is what distinguishes the genius from the little artist who
creates only to create and imitates only to imitate, who
is quite content himself with the minor satisfactions of
technique, makes this technique his sole aim, and

requires that we also shall be content with just that same sort of minor satisfaction which arises from his artistic but purposeless exercise of his technique.

And to the same effect, were it not otiose to do so, it would be possible to cite the criticism of every age which has had a great literature; while a lack of sense for this *"sorte de lieu commun moral"* is an almost infallible sign of critical and literary decadence. For life is to us a moral affair; and if literature succeeds in its purpose of representing life, its perusal, like experience, will result in the attachment of correct values to human action, not because it is the business of literature to inculcate morals, but because it is the business of literature to represent life, and life is a moral affair. The mere stylist like Gautier is felt to be less than first-rate, in spite of the seduction of his manner, simply because he has no great ideas of human life to commemorate.

But this is very different from expecting a novel to be written for the promotion of social or religious doctrine or for the exploitation of theories or hypotheses of any kind. To attempt to use literature for such a purpose, or to require of it the solution of philosophical problems, is evidence of a strange perversion on the part of writer or critic. Philosophies are at best fluctuating and transitory; they change from generation to generation. The consequences of human action are alone of eternal interest to the human kind. And he who builds beyond the moment must build not upon the former but upon the latter. Nor do such ideas, as a rule or as an exception, afford a just measure for the evaluation of human life. On the contrary, they tend to force life and its expression into narrow, ready-made equations, true enough for the day but by so much the falser for the morrow; in other words, to reduce it temporarily to order by the summary process of strait-jacketing it. One attempting the representation, or better the interpretation, of life, ought to bring to its study no preconceived ideas. All such ideas should, where they enter literature at all, be strictly distinguished as foreign to its purpose—that is, as extra-literary. They may not always be impertinent or uninteresting, but they are subordinate and inessential; and where they rise into prominence and importance above the life of the book, they are so,—both impertinent and uninteresting from the point of view of literature. And yet there are those who pretend to read a novel for nothing more than its historical background, or its treatment of a political issue or some other vexed question. In spite of the modern popularisation of literature—perhaps its vulgarisation,—one has not ceased to recommend Scott for the historical information to be got

out of him, or George Eliot for her curious
cases of moral casuistry, or Mrs. Ward for her
religious disputation;—clearly literary imperti-
nences in any case and not the vitality that
gives these writers their strength.

The best training for a novelist is not a system
but an experience—a first-hand knowledge
of men and their ways acquired from the give
and take of existence, where the hard facts,
by dint of battering the consciousness, finally
gain recognition. This is the open school in
which the novelist best learns his lesson, not
in the cloisters of a creed. It is here he learns
of human responsibility, of the consequences
of human action, of the fatality of the human
will; here he learns "what life and death is";
and here finally he gets his ideas of the world
direct from the world itself, not in set formulæ
or generalised prescriptions, but embedded
in the tissue of individual examples by which
he conveys them to others. Literature can
never be studied from any mirrored image,
not even from literature itself, without distortion
or conventionality. Some arrangements of
facts he must make, no doubt; but these are
not the classifications of a rigid system, they
are the peculiarities of flesh and blood.

Such was George Sand's training. It is well
understood now that she belonged to no sect,
accepted no creeds, held no tenets or dogmas,

literary or otherwise, which might have controlled her at the outset though at the risk of cramping her early genius. But unfortunately, while she began writing solely from her experience and observation, she began at a moment of violent reaction and revolt, when her feelings were still running riot with her reason. And this circumstance imparted to her first work, together with a spirit of reality and naturalness hitherto wanting to French fiction, a wildness and incoherence that marred the product. The naturalness and reality, for which she had her observation and experience to thank, gave her instant popularity, her writer's capital at the start; while her revolt produced the mental and moral confusion of her first period.

Free of creeds and dogmas as she naturally was, she could have met with nothing more unlucky for the development of her genius than that, almost immediately, and before her literary character was formed, she should have fallen under the influence of those who were essentially theorisers and *doctrinaires*. An admirer of Rousseau from the first, with an obscure bias in her nature toward a hazy humanitarianism, she devoted the production of her second period, inspired by her masculine friendships and attachments, to the ill-advised attempt to make the novel an instrument of social reform. No one can doubt that her enthusiasm over Lamennais' Christian communism was sincere for the moment, but equally so for another moment was her admiration for Pierre Leroux's socialism, and for still another her interest in freemasonry. The fact is that these notions for which she was momentarily inspired were never hers by origination and that she never made them so by adoption. The personal weight of those who professed them imposed them upon her feminine susceptibility; and with the artist's impulsiveness she worked them off upon her novels. Naturally her presentation of them was confused and uncertain. And the result is much the same with other novels of hers of this and other periods, which are not strictly *Tendenz* perhaps but may be fairly classed together with the preceding as extra-literary, since they were not written under purely literary inspiration or with purely literary motives, and since—the most important test—who reads them reads them primarily for something over and above their literary interest —for the side-light generally which they throw upon the life, character, or thought of their author or of her time. "I have found," says Coleridge, and the remark is as true of the novel as it is of poetry, "that where the subject is taken immediately from the author's personal sensations and experiences, the excellence of a particular poem is but an equivocal mark, and often a fallacious pledge, of genuine poetic power." Woman as she was, her feelings when aroused were ever of a vehemence to overbalance her critical judgment; and in writing for the gratification of these feelings rather than from the instinct of letters she was likely, no matter at what time of life, to reproduce the emotional confusion of her earliest period. A remark that she herself makes in her memoirs concerning *le Piccinino* is significant in this connection, and justifies in closing as well as illustrates my use of the word "extra-literary" as a general designation for all this kind of work. "*Ce que je pense de la noblesse de race, je l'ai écrit dans le Piccinino*," she says, "*et je n'ai peut-être fait ce roman que pour faire les trois chapitres où j'ai dévelloppé mon sentiment sur la noblesse.*" It is often so, too often, in fact, that the purpose of her novels early and late, as she confesses here, is to be sought and found outside of character, situation, and plot.

De Musset himself, whatever else he may or may not have stood for, was one of the few exclusively literary ascendencies to which she ever submitted. He it was who awoke her to the existence of such a thing as form and taught her all she ever learned, except of herself, about style. It is impossible to estimate how

great was the detriment to her genius that she
should have been so long under influences that,
while intellectual, were in no sense literary, and
should have been obliged to work her way alone
out of much that was harmful to her spirit.
Had her flow been less full and copious, it may
well be questioned whether the stream would
not have choked in the sands of sociological
and metaphysical discussion with which she
was surrounded, and she have ended where
George Eliot began, as a mere controversialist.
It is not a little singular that these two women,
the greatest *littératrices* of their respective coun-
tries, should both have been for a time under the
dominance of inspirations other than literary,
and should have been more or less diverted
from their proper paths and more or less hindered in their proper activities by philosophical
speculation.   Of the two, George Eliot was more
inclined to such thought, and never, indeed, got
quite clear of the clutter of erudition, while
George Sand was in reality of no great philosophical bent and never assimilated such ideas
thoroughly enough to handle them with firmness.

As a result of her feeble grasp of such subjects
and of the vivacity of her feelings, she was at
her best when she centred her novels neither
in a doctrinal *motif* nor a merely personal emotion, but in some simple episode of common life
which she had noticed and been touched by.

Her masterpieces are few in number—as any one's must be—but they are perfect in their kind:—*la Mare au diable, la Petite Fadette, François le champi. Les Maîtres sonneurs*, of the same attempt as the others, errs by excessive development; it overreaches and out-runs itself and in spite of much good grows wearisome by its length; while *Jeanne* and the *Meunier d'Angibault*, which are sometimes classed with these, show traces of confusion due partly to the introduction of extra-literary ideas and partly to the mixture of idyllic and social elements; so that none of these latter three can be ranked as masterpieces beside the former. Her own district of Berri, which she always loved and to which she returned more and more in later life, furnished her with the setting for these flawless gems. After the welter of passions and ideas, into which she had been cast young and in which she was long whirled, had subsided, and she could attend to the voice of her own desires; when her love of the unaffected and the natural asserted itself and she had leisure for quiet contemplation in the face of nature;—then she was quick to recognise and respond to the charm of just such characters and incidents as she met in her *Vallée noire* of the romantic name, and as she has rendered with exquisite sensibility. The simple, unpretentious life of the peasant amid

his fields with his robust loves and hates, hopes
and fears, was a discovery in comparative
humanity to French letters. The healthfulness
and freshness of these idyls, full of the air of
wood and lawn, the breath of morning and
evening, is a revelation after the stale intrigue
skulking away in the close and tainted atmosphere of city rooms. They justify to the English
reader the existence of French fiction. It may
be, as M. Brunetière declares, that George
Sand made the French novel capable of sustaining thought; it is of infinitely greater credit to
her to have shown that it was possible for the
French novel to carry good, clean, wholesome
sentiment. No reader of modern French
fiction can return to these stories without feeling
that there life, as well as literature, has been
triumphantly vindicated against *naturalism*,
and without feeling, too, that his heart has been
purified and gladdened by contact with a
simple and sincere art.

ZOLA

MR. VIZETELLY'S account of Zola[1] is at all events the best in the language. And indeed, though decidedly partial and unnecessarily obstructed with "shop," it is by no means an unserviceable or uninteresting book. Mr. Vizetelly is a "journalist." As foreign correspondent of the London papers he has spent a good deal of time in Paris and is thoroughly acquainted with the life, habits, and habitat of the *gens de lettres* and with the ins and outs of the literary business. His father's was one of the first English houses to venture upon the publication of Zola to any extent; and latterly he himself has served as the novelist's interpreter and intermediary, and has enjoyed in that capacity some degree of intimacy with his principal. As a source of information, then, as a collection of fact, anecdote, and detail, the biography may be considered as authoritative as anything we have, though it suffers from one serious drawback, the uneventfulness and tedium of modern authorship.

Zola was born at Paris, April 2, 1840; he

[1] *Émile Zola, Novelist and Reformer*. By E. A. Vizetelly. New York: John Lane.

was married in 1869: and he was suffocated
by a defective flue, September 29, 1902.   He was
brought up in Aix, the "Plassans" of his novels,
whence his family moved to Paris in 1853
in dire poverty, his father being then dead and
his affairs in disorder.   There Émile continued
his education, probably at some sacrifice on the
part of the remainder of the family.   He failed
however, to take his degree at Paris, and again
at Marseilles, where he made a second attempt
after his first failure at the capital.   For a few
years he beat about the city in penury, until
he obtained employment with Hachette, the
publisher, with whom he remained until he had
obtained a pretty firm footing in journalism.
From this point his biography becomes nearly
identical with the history of his writings, that
stupendous encyclopedia of human vice, which
engrossed him for the rest of his life.   The most
exceptional incident of his later career was his
vigorous interference in the Dreyfuss affair.
For the rest he spent his spare time talking
shop with his colleagues, dined with them
occasionally, inhabited Médan in summer and
Paris in winter.   In striking contrast with
artistic tradition, with the romance of a Cellini
or a Goethe, his life was largely a matter of
business, made up of engagements with news-
papers and journals, of contracts with *éditeurs*
and theatrical managers, of incomings and

expenses. But then Zola had no pretensions to art; what he pretended to, ridiculously enough, was science.

As for his ancestry the ethnologist, or whoever looks after such matters, may detect some significance in the mixture of his blood—Italian on the father's, French on the mother's side. But more important, probably, for the determination of his genius were the circumstances of his bringing up. As an "artist" his most inveterate trait is his insensibility to beauty; for what he failed to observe is the fact that in spite of his pretensions to science his work is by no means a record of facts at all but a piece of lurid and sinister impressionism. It is as much of a selection as that of any other writer; but it is a selection of the base, the ignoble, and the hideous, And to this infection of ugliness which corrupts his novels, it must be confessed, he was early exposed. His school days at Aix appear the pleasantest of his life, certainly the pleasantest to dwell on; though wretched enough, they were not without something of the wholesome idealism which ought to form the atmosphere of youth. At all events he got a little fresh air and saw something of the country, and even, it seems, caught a fleeting glimpse of romance and poetry, saw the goddess in going. Unlovely enough in contrast, though more in-fluential upon his future, were the days of his

5

early obscurity in Paris, where he seems to have
fribbled away his time, in a manner not uncommon to French youth, in dingy dissipation,
studying half-heartedly or moping in a garret
with some creature of the pavement.   To the
English taste fortunately there is still something
inexpressibly shabby about such a literary
apprenticeship and the fruit it usually brings
forth.

Les vers se sent toujours des bassesses du cœur.

Critically, however, it must be confessed that
Mr. Vizetelly's book is rather feeble.   It has little
literary discernment, still less literary principle.
Above all it suffers from the limitation which
is at once the quality and defect of journalism
—contemporaneity.   It fails to see Zola as a
whole and it fails to see him from without.   At
the same time it leaves one phase of his character
altogether unlighted—and that the most suggestive and symptomatic.   For to any unpreju-
diced student of his mind it is abundantly
evident that he must have been subject to
curious delusions.   There is a kind of cloud about
his spirit like that which envelops Ibsen's and
Tolstoi's, impenetrable by ordinary methods of
divination.   For the reader, therefore, who
would form a complete idea of Zola and his
significance, Mr. Vizetelly's account requires
to be supplemented by the impressions of some

critical acquaintance, whose impressions in turn should be checked and controlled by a general sense of literature as a whole. For such an estimate the materials are fortunately at hand.

On December 2, 1851, the very day of Louis Napoleon's *coup d'état*, two Parisians, brothers and collaborators, Edmond and Jules de Goncourt, began a sort of diary for the commemoration of their literary experience. Jules, the younger, died in 1870; but Edmond continued the work alone until his own death in 1896. Jotted down hastily after the events of the day, full of colloquialism and slang, indifferent even to grammar, careful only to reproduce the vividness of the original impression, these notes, which run to the length of nine printed volumes, are remarkable as forming a continuous personal chronicle of French letters for a period of very nearly half a century. The writers were preoccupied exclusively with literature; with Flaubert they make an instance almost unique of men living solely in literature. Politics, public events, the great march of human history had no place in their interests, or in their journal hardly so much as a mention. But in compensation they were intimate with all the great French writers of their time; and them they have transferred to the pages of their record with a relentlessness almost photographic,

abusing the privilege of familiar intercourse to
catch them in all sorts of unguarded and not
infrequently compromising attitudes. Whatever may be thought of the delicacy of such
a proceeding, there is no gainsaying that the
results are intensely interesting and often valuable in completing the portrait of some celeb-
rity whom we should know otherwise but
indifferently.

Of all that brilliant coterie of writers which
makes up the main concern of these nine volumes, Zola was the last survivor. When he died
not so very long ago, there passed away, not
only the last great power of French letters,
but also the last inheritor of a long tradition.
Maupassant, Daudet, Gautier, Goncourt, even
the vociferous Flaubert, the "master," he
knew them all. He had foregathered with them
at their famous little dinners, and he had borne
his part in the conversations which furnished
Goncourt with so much of his material—
vinous, heady, after-dinner talk, but brilliant
withal and full of marrow. And he had had
his share with them in that sweeping movement,
of which each represented a particular interest
and whose upshot was the deformation of the
novel.

From the pages of this familiar record, therefore, it is not very difficult for a reader with some
sense of literary values to derive a clear con-

ception of Zola's person and private character.
Under the date of January 25, 1875, Goncourt
makes the following significant observation.

Zola continued to groan. When we told him that
he had nothing to complain of and had made pretty
good way for a man not yet thirty-five, he exclaimed:
"Shall I speak from the bottom of my heart? You 'll
think me a baby; but so much the worse—I shall
never be decorated, I shall never belong to the
Academy, I shall never have a distinction to certify to
my talent. In the eyes of the public I shall always
be a pariah." And he repeated it four or five times,
"A pariah."

In the light of the present the remark seems
singularly clear-sighted, almost prophetic. The
best and most reputable opinion, whether
instinctive or critical, has always looked at Zola
a little askance, in spite of his tremendous
influence, and will probably continue to do so.
Even Anatole France, who ended by pronouncing
his eulogy, had found but little good to say
of his work in the heyday of his success, and
was drawn to him finally rather by force of
social and political, than of literary, sympathy.
His very name stirs a sort of instinctive antagonism even in those who would divest themselves
of academic as well as of popular prejudices.
Untimely as he died, he had yet lived long enough
to see his old friends and familiars perish and
their systems with them, to see his own school
and formula discredited and himself repudiated

by his own disciples. And his case had this additional bitterness. Whereas his colleagues, even the Goncourts, had left at least some small residuum of work to outlive their theorising, a single masterpiece like Flaubert's if no more; he must have had reason to doubt sometimes whether his own immense labour, tainted as it was with the vices of his generation and his own errors, had not abutted in nothing, whether it had amounted to a single volume of permanent literary value. For I confess I can not imagine any one, unaffected by the momentary prepossessions and prejudices of our own age, reading Zola for any other motive than one of irrelevant curiosity. To the sociologist so called, to the student of manners, to the historian he may continue to be of some documentary interest; but to the permanent acquisitions of the human spirit, to culture, he has made no lasting contribution. And that Zola himself had come to understand, or at all events to feel, his ultimate failure, notwithstanding the dust he had raised, seems evident enough from the attempt he made some years ago to wrench his work into a new direction—an attempt, for all its vigour, at once grotesque and pitiable.

The curious perversity of his character, his irritability, his singular insubordination to discipline, his contempt of tradition, which marred

so many of his qualities and which make him
at all times so irritating and occasionally so
contemptible—these are already noticeable in
Goncourt's account of their first meeting, December 14, 1868, in an entry which brings the
reader into the immediate presence of the past
as though it were written but yesterday. Zola
was then twenty-eight, still struggling for
money and recognition, still in the grip of that
iron necessity which he never ceased to hate and
against which he was always in a state of more
or less open mutiny.

To-day we had our admirer Zola to breakfast. . . .
Viewed closely this vigorous young man seemed to
have certain delicacies, like modellings of fine porce-
lain, in the features of his face, the chiselling of his eye-
lids, the curious flatnesses of his nose; his whole person
cut, in short, after the fashion of the characters of his
books, those complex creatures, rather feminine for
all their virility.

Then one of his striking sides is the morbid, sickly,
ultra-nervous side, which impresses you at times with
the poignant sensation of sitting by a melancholic and
rebellious victim of heart disease.

In a word an uneasy, anxious, profound, complicated,
elusive, illegible sort of man.

He told us about his difficulties, of his desire and need
of a publisher to buy him for six years at 30,000 francs
and so assure him 6000 francs a year, bread for his
mother and himself, thereby giving him a chance to
write *The History of a Family*, a novel in eight volumes.
For he would like to make "big machines." No more
of these "infamous, ignoble" articles he cried in a tone

of self-contempt. . . . Then after a silence: "The fact
is, I have so many enemies—and it 's so hard to get
oneself talked about."

And from time to time he would break out into bitter
recriminations, repeating to us and himself that he was
only twenty-eight, with a note of acrid resolution and
passionate energy.

Very much as he appeared in this first inter-
view with the Goncourts, he remained to the
end. Egotistic he was, it will have been seen,
tormented by the itch of notoriety, wrong-
headed, defiant, nursing a grudge against
society, but not the worst of friends, perhaps,
and worthy of sympathy in his early struggles
to support his mother and family—struggles,
alas! in which he was forced to surrender many
of the nicer feelings which he had the taste to
admire without the resolution to ensue. But
however we may like him personally—whatever
we may think of his criticism of his contemporaries in the columns of the Russian magazines,
a proceeding which was characterised by
other than its victims as a prostitution of his
pen and a treachery to his order and which was
in any case a good stroke of business; whether
we see in his conduct in the Dreyfus affair
a single devotion to justice, an outbreak of
his old rebelliousness at existing conditions, or
merely another attack of his mania of *réclame*
—however, in short, we take him as a man, it

must be acknowledged that he had at all events
the one sad virtue of his courage, whatever
his convictions, and that with Ibsen and Tolstoi
he has had an extraordinary effect, not merely
on the literature of his own country, but upon
that of the whole civilised world. Indeed if
he were to be estimated solely by the extent
and immediacy of his influence, he would take
an easy pre-eminence as one of the very greatest
writers that ever lived. In the space of a
single lifetime he has overturned the whole
conception of the novel, and along with it the
entire spiritual habit and temper on which it
rested; and in so doing he has naturally modified the whole modern outlook upon life to such
an extent that the present attitude to art and
nature would probably be all but unintelligible
to such a dabster of letters as our old friend
of comfortable views and easy-going romance,
Sir Walter Scott. So unprecedented, as a
matter of fact, has been his infectiousness, even
in this age of sudden and tremendous reputa-
tions, that it stands out as the most striking
singularity of his career and crucially significant
of his literary character. For it is his willingness
to follow the lead of his generation, to fall in with
its tendencies, to which he was remarkably
sensitive though he was not always capable
of comprehending them, his readiness to serve
as a mouthpiece to whatever was fermenting

obscurely in the heart of the time, to which his
success was due.

In the first place, the pretension to found a
literature entirely upon observation could hardly
fail to flatter an age conspicuously lacking in
imagination; while in eyes insensible to literary
values and accustomed to look upon fiction of the
older sort as frivolous, the "documentary"
character of the new novel would serve as a
guarantee of its positive practical worth. At
the same time the proposal to study life nakedly
and without evasion, at its worst as at its best,
was one that appealed irresistibly to the new
spirit of fearless curiosity and honest investi-
gation which was then prevailing and which,
however it has been abused and exploited, was
and still is a spirit worthy only of commendation
in itself. To these professions, it should not be
forgotten, Zola's style lent a specious credita-
bility — those hard sharp evocations of brutal
physical fact like something scratched on
flint, those horrid physiological and moral
stigmata—in a word, that whole pitiless dis-
embowelling of life and the dangling of its convulsive viscera before the agonised spectators,
which was eminently characteristic of the
school and was felt, just in proportion to its
crudity, to be "real" and "scientific."

And yet preposterous as the idea of "scientific
fiction" actually was, thus much of science,

if one stickle for the name, may be allowed
his novels. Properly understood, they have
little or none of that personal significance which
constitutes the interest of literature. They
centre, not upon an individual, but upon some
nebulous "social complex" such as the speculation of the time was already beginning dimly
to conceive—a community, a profession, a class
which the writer "gets up" like a reporter
supplying his paper with "copy." There is no
particular hero to *la Débâcle;* the protagonist
is the army or France itself, breathless, pros-
trate, before whose agony the personal element
fades into insignificance. Or even more vaguely
and abstractly it is a symbol, a mere figure of
war, as Zola himself calls it. For in the thought
of his day the integrity of the human soul has
given way before some vague abstraction of
"social forces," which overrides the individual
and inhibits his personal influence ; while
humanitarianism is no longer a sympathy with
one's fellows in the great common tragedy
of life, but a dim, diffusive, bewildered consciousness of one's own image brokenly reflected
in the "social organism," as a wave might
see itself, if it had vision, mirrored distortedly
in the ocean, of which it is a helpless and undifferentiated portion, And so the novel in
Zola's hands becomes a *compte-rendu*, a report
of social conditions, a sociological thesis.

And yet if this had been all there was to him, it is doubtful whether he would ever have made so profound an impression as he actually did make upon his contemporaries at home and abroad. But his work had power; and power, however sadly it may be misapplied, is sure of its affair. The actual labour in units of work required to make a book is so great that he who would sustain it must be thoroughly convinced that it is worth while or else must be of a remarkably sanguine temperament. But as the world grows less and less naïve, less and less childishly ingenuous and self-confident, authorship tends increasingly to become less and less a matter of taste and more and more a matter of industry and energy, as Zola was shrewd enough to recognise. "It is only by the quantity of one's work," Goncourt reports him as saying, "the power of one's creation, that one can appeal to the public nowadays." And about a year later Goncourt writes: "Zola works every day from nine to half-past twelve and from three to eight. This he must do even now with talent, almost fame, in order to earn his bread." Indeed, so tremendous is his application that it affects his health. He is troubled with vapours and formless misgivings; he sees ghosts; his work becomes an incubus, a nightmare. He is no longer master of his thought but mastered by it.

Zola came to see me to-day. He entered with the

lugubrious and haggard manner which characterises
his entrances. He sank into a chair complaining
almost childishly of pains in his reins . . . and pal-
pitations of the heart. Then he spoke of the death
of his mother . . . And when he began to talk of
literature and what he wished to do, he let slip his
dread lest he should not have the time for it.

Here, then, is the proper portrait of the
modern author—a labourer like another, plying
his trade at scheduled hours day in, day out,
the slave of his business, if not its victim,
subdued to what he works in, respected more
for the size of his "output" and the quantity of
his editions than for their quality and that of
their readers. It is no longer the man who is,
the man of assured elective genius led by natural
propensity, but the man who strives and struggles to be—*forcierte Talente*, as Goethe calls
them. And with the change there begins also
a new literature, the kind of thing to which
a man of common abilities and uncommon
diligence may reasonably aspire—a literature
reflecting its maker's peculiarities, like him
wanting in creative imagination and inter-
pretative insight, very strong in the practical
imitative sense, sticking close to fact as it is—
a literature essentially democratic in its hostility to the elevation and distinction inherent
in the old conception of letters as an affair of
gift and cultivated feeling—a literature, in short,

singularly acceptable to the modern consciousness as open without further qualification to
whoever has the patience and endurance to
undergo it. In the antagonism which has always
existed between the life contemplative and the
life active, between the artist and the Philistine,
we are confronted in Zola's work with the depressing spectacle of the triumph, at least temporary, of the latter over the former on what
was once thought its own exclusive territory.

Nor does it help matters much to remember
that in this, as in all that Zola does, there is a
touch of charlatanry, of that double consciousness which enters in varying degrees into the
character of the parasite, the courtier, and the
politician. He knows the insincerity of his
pretensions at the same time that he pretends
with conviction, and he is not above acknow-
ledging it to one who has penetrated his secret.
It is like getting behind the scenes to the
illusion of the whole comedy to read in Goncourt
the retort he makes to an attack of Flaubert's,
who was always ridiculing his talk about "naturalism."

" You! " exclaims Zola. " You have a little fortune
of your own, which has enabled you to keep clear of a
great many unpleasantnesses. But as for me—
I 've been forced to earn my bread entirely by my
pen. I 've had to make my way by all sorts of writings—yes, all sorts of contemptible writings. Good
Heavens! I despise this word 'naturalism' as much

as you do. But I shall go on using it, because things must have a name if the public is to believe they 're new. . . .

"First, I 've fixed a nail, and with a blow of my hammer I 've driven it into the public's skull an inch; then with a second blow I 've driven it in another inch. Well, my hammer is the journalism I do for myself in connection with my own works."

Lo! our portrait of the modern author stands completed by his own hand. In addition to his other activities, he humbugs the ingenuous public with a name or some other "good hooraw"—

> " thet 's wut the people likes;
> Sutthin' combinin' morril truth with phrases sech ez strikes "—

and with the assistance of his own disinterested criticism, anonymously published, he gradually succeeds in working himself up a very pretty notoriety.

The fact is that Zola's is a puzzling, enigmatical sort of personality, and in that respect, as in so many others, representative of his times. There was undoubtedly at the bottom of his make-up a stratum of honesty, courage, and good faith. But like other men deficient in the highest culture and discipline he must have lived in a constant hallucination. I lay no particular stress in this connection on his determination to ugliness or on his belief in an organised conspiracy to ruin him, which are usually reckoned as symptoms of mental alienation.   As a matter of fact I do not suppose that Zola was madder than are most of us.   What I refer to is that form of delusion which consists in believing that things are other than they are, or that, being as they are, their results will be other than they will be, simply because it is we who have to do with them.   And to this form of hallucination he was particularly susceptible. Just as he could persuade himself, for instance, that this "naturalism" of his, whose nakedness he should one day expose to his intimates, was something of the noblest after all, and could still later, when profitable, turn square about to work for the most vapid socialistic idealism that ever floated by its own levity between heaven and earth in the region of the impalpable inane; just so he had no difficulty in believing that his enormous circulation was due solely to literary merit, when all the time he must have been conscious in some way or other that it was due in reality to his flattery of the lowest and most subterraneous instincts of human nature.

In the first petition for *Tartuffe* Molière boasts with legitimate pride that he has left in the play nothing morally ambiguous, nothing that might tend to confuse the distinction between good and evil.   The principle is as

sound to-day as it was then; and much as we
may shut our eyes to the consequences, its
violation is attended with inevitable harm.
For whoever attempts to introduce into literature anything that is itself equivocal or that
tends to confuse this distinction, does not only
debase the art that he is practising, but also
throws away one of the strongest and most vital
motives at his command—the absorbing conflict
between good and evil. He fails to present a
sound conception of life; he fails to inspire us
with those correct ideas whose acquirement
is the end of experience; and, what is perhaps
equally or even more to the point as far as he
is concerned, he fails to interest us and arouse
our enthusiasm as he might have done. For
after all the ultimate significance of existence
is interpreted by our conscience and our moral
nature. To live is not only to have engaged
ourselves in the struggle of right and wrong,
but to have learned the difference between them.
But it was one of the faults of Zola's contemporaries to make this very confusion. And
in following their lead here as elsewhere, he has
sacrificed to an immediate vogue the permanent
position to which his powers might otherwise
have entitled him—provided he had the moral
sense for it, for that is the very question his
novels leave unanswered.

6

JONATHAN SWIFT

LUDIBRIUM RERUM HUMANARUM

THE virtual completion of Mr. Temple
Scott's new edition of Swift's prose
writings[1] naturally invites to a reconsideration
of the strangely perturbed and intemperate
spirit of which they are at once the mask and
the expression. To be sure, something like a
definitive edition of his poetry and his correspondence would be desirable also. But so
much of his work is contained between the
covers of these volumes that it is hardly pre-
sumptuous to attempt to pronounce upon him
on the strength of this freshly bolted material
alone.

I

On the whole Swift belongs to that small
class of authors whose character is more arrest-
ing and significant than the main bulk of their
work. There is a natural temptation for a
critic or editor to exalt the object of his atten-

[1] *The Prose Works of Jonathan Swift, D.D.* Edited
by Temple Scott. 12 vols. Bohn's Library. New York:
The Macmillan Co.

tions; and Mr. Scott, like other exhibitors of Swift, is inclined to take rather too bright a view of the latter's authorship. In literature, as in many other respects, Swift was a man of his age, and, as will be seen, not always of the best, or at least of the prevailing, tendencies of that age. And in spite of the fact that it was the nursery of modern English, the prose ideal of that particular period was after all a very imperfect one. It was well enough in affirming the virtues of clearness, simplicity, and reason. But it erred in attempting to follow too closely the misleading example of talk, and it fell in consequence into shallowness and commonplace. It failed to go deep enough, it fetched up no profound moral ideas. And only a century later, after Johnson had succeeded in pioneering a general reaction, did English prose find itself properly headed, with many of its lost powers restored, on the road to Burke and the great modern masters of style. In its kind Swift's prose is both more and less satisfactory than Addison's. While it is much less "elegant" and academic, it is much more searching and racy. But at the same time it is Addison's finish and "correctness" which have made him classic, while Swift's poignancy and liveliness are results of his nearer approach to that "timeliness," that "occasionalism" which has served only to

disable so much of the work of his contemporaries. For just as there was never an age
more factious and insular, so there was never
a literature as a whole more local, more temporal in its subjects and its appeal, more dependent for its interest upon a knowledge of
contemporary circumstance, than that of
Anne. And, paradoxically enough, this very
hindrance has always constituted its fascination
for those who most affect it. It is so partial
that one who would know it at all must know
it whole, both in itself, that is, and in its relation to society. But this sort of interest,
which has led Leslie Stephen into an imprudent
extension of critical generalities true only of
the early eighteenth century, is not of the
purest alloy nor of the most lasting substance.
And it is not difficult to see that in conforming
to the fashion, both in style and in subject,
Swift's prose, good as it is after its kind, does
represent a false, or at least a losing ideal in
literature, just as his political opinions represent
such another in politics.

II

For his statesmanship, frequently condemned
as it has been, there is one line of apology which
I have never seen taken, capable though it
appears of specious and even brilliant defence.
It would not be impossible, perhaps, for a

skilful casuist to maintain that Swift, though out of joint with the general political movement of his time, was, on the whole, perfectly right in his ideas, that the measures which he advocated were, in spite of the discredit cast upon them in the outcome, the measures most expedient for England at that particular juncture. In favour of such a contention there is much to be urged. Whatever their motives, the Tories of Swift's party stood for peace, for conformity, for unrestricted trade; and surely these are liberal ideas as compared with the narrow Chauvinism of the Whigs in all that concerned war and commerce, to say nothing of that cultivation of factiousness in religion and politics which was a characteristic feature of their management. Nay, it might be possible for such an advocate as I have supposed to go farther, even to assert with some show of plausibility that, dazzled by Macaulay's "eloquent commonplace," we have in many instances come to mistake the course of development since Swift's day for altogether desirable because it happens to be actual. But however this may be, it is certain that he himself was in direct and violent opposition to the ideas which were, as a matter of fact, fated to obtain in Church and State. And this opposition, which was almost exactly coterminous with his interests, is capital for the estimation of his temper, because it was itself mainly instrumental in determining the particular trait of character upon which his significance as man and writer chiefly depends. For it was his extreme sensibility which, played upon by circumstances and exasperated by failure, became the source, not merely of all that is thwart and perverse, but also of all that is permanent and valuable in his life and writings.

III

With respect to his sensibility the case is indeed a peculiar one. For all his sagacity and hard-headedness, it is amazing and pathetic, too, the fatality with which he invariably arrayed himself on the off-side. The dupe of his own prejudices and not infrequently of his own self-conceit, he was egregiously deceived in almost all his friends. While he believed himself settled in the confidence of Harley and St. John, they were hoodwinking him to the top of their bent, and, deep in treasonable correspondence with the Pretender, were allowing him to cover them with his own credit at the risk of his personal safety and of his reputation with posterity. Even Pope, who had no political designs to excuse his private perfidies, took advantage of his old companion's failing mind, for the benefit of his own miserable literary ambition, in one of the dirtiest tricks

ever recorded, I hope, of a man of letters. Nor
is the fatuity much less, it would appear, with
which he mistook the general trend and upshot
of the period—with which, in short, he miscon-
ceived society and his own relation to it. In
this respect he stands in the most striking
contrast with another figure of the day, the
cool, circumspect, successful Addison, who
seems to have caught the trick of getting on in
the world as Swift had missed it. "I believe
if he had a mind to be chosen King he could
hardly be refused," wrote the latter in witness
of his popularity; while he himself, on his return
as dean to Ireland, "was hustled and pelted
in the streets," and for some months "never
ventured to show himself even in the principal
thoroughfares without an escort of armed
servants."

But swayed as he was by his feelings, the
effort which he made to suppress or deny them
is hardly less remarkable. He hated hypocrisy;
but he had made himself over in its inverted
image rather than incur the sentimental odium
of his own virtues. For much as he detested
pretence, he was thoroughly ashamed of "enthusiasm," and had rather belie his best and
noblest instincts than incur the reproach of it.
The stories of his secret charities, his stealthy
benefactions, his stifled prayers, which have
leaked out with time, make a sad record of

improvidence in a world where lights are not
usually kindled under bushels.   In its glacial
rigidity, its assumed and despairing restraint,
no more affecting utterance was ever penned
than the "Character of Mrs. Johnson":

This day, being Sunday, January 28, 1727/8, about
eight o'clock at night, a servant brought me a note,
with an account of the death of the truest, most virtuous, and valuable friend, that I, or perhaps any other
person, was ever blessed with.   She expired about
six in the evening of this day;   and as soon as I am
left alone, which is about eleven at night, I resolve,
for my own satisfaction, to say something of her life
and character.   .   .   .
This is the night of the funeral, which my sickness
will not suffer me to attend.   It is now nine at night,
and I am removed into another apartment, that I may
not see the light in the church, which is just over against
the window of my bedchamber.

No man may quarrel with his age with
impunity.   Contemporaries may be in error, but
to break with them is not only to lose his one
chance of spiritual catholicity and to invite
material defeat;   it is also to introduce a
principle of infection into his own *morale*.
But upon such a nature as this of Swift's
it is obvious that defection must have had a
singularly cankering effect;   it is remarkable
that it should not have had a thoroughly de-
moralising one.

IV

In regard to the man himself, it is impossible to enter very far into his character without some brief preliminary consideration of his relationship with Stella—that vexed question concerning which there has been "so much throwing about of brains." And yet the matter seems fairly simple after all. One of his earliest and strongest resolutions was to allow of no entanglement that might stand in the way of his career. But of all such entanglements there was none that struck him as more fatal, none at which he railed more scornfully (only, perhaps, because he was chiding his own rebellious inclinations) than this of an imprudent marriage. Besides, it is possible to detect in his inordinate ambition, in his impatience to establish himself, and the long odds he was willing to take of fortune, the wish to satisfy a desire which was not heroic enough to jump at the bait and suffer the consequences. He was too clear-sighted, too sensitive to penury and sordidness and dependence—above all, to ridicule —to make any such step. And this combination of speculative vehemence and practical calculation is one of his most marked characteristics. But as his hopes were dashed again and again, as he found himself confirming in failure, the habit of restraint grew upon a nature

congenitally dubitative in action, until, seeing
himself frustrated and beaten at forty-five,
he lacked the heart and the habit to do other
than he had been doing all his life.   It was no
longer possible to change the crease so long and
painfully folded into his consciousness.

This seems as clear and simple as can reasonably be expected of Swift.   But the view
gains plausibility from a comparison of his
conduct on other occasions.   Most curious and
indicative of all is his behaviour on his return
to London immediately after his preferment
to the deanery of St. Patrick's.   Recalled to
the assistance of his friends and party who are
in division and on the edge of ruin, he abandons
them to their fate, retires into the country,
and occupies himself with his recollections and
literary amusements.

I am now retired into the country, he writes,
weary to death of courts and ministers and business
and politics.   And to Arbuthnot: You are a set of
people drawn almost to the dregs; you must try
another game; this is at an end.   Your ministry is
fourscore and ten years old [in reality, it may have
been about half a dozen], and all you can endeavour
at is a euthanasia.

This singular apathy, this sense of disillusion
and emptiness and vanity, which has evidently
supervened upon his former energy and enthusiasm, is thoroughly symptomatic of his mental

constitution. With everything he touched there came a time, sooner or later, when it seemed to drop to pieces under his hands. The glory, the glamour of possible achievement faded out before his very eyes and left him, still dazzled, but vacant, listless, and disabused. It may be that the root of such disenchantment was partly physiological (though it is necessary to give up the idea that his insanity was in any way constitutional); probably it was in great part moral, a kind of *défaillance*, an obscure treachery of body and mind, which began by betraying, and ended by vitiating, the active will. Something of such a *crise* is perceptible now and then in his writings below that long-drawn falsetto of exasperation and despair which has since become so frequent in literature.

Nor is this, in fact, his sole likeness with decadence. There are moments when he seems to have anticipated, by nearly two centuries, Ibsen and Tolstoy and all that degenerate late-nineteenth-century crew, as curiously, though not by quite so long an interval, as did Shakespeare in his *Troilus and Cressida* and his *Measure for Measure*. Like them he is almost totally insensible to beauty of any kind. To his mind the one significant and over-powering aspect of the world is its hideousness. He is not merely disturbed and shocked, he is literally hag-ridden by it. Seldom or never

can he see anything else—certainly never
anything else so distinctly and consistently.
"All the virtues that have been in mankind,"
he declares, "are to be counted upon a few
fingers, but follies and vices are innumerable
and time adds hourly to the heap." Even
his sententious and aphoristic philosophy is but
the wisdom of the burnt child and the sick
stomach. "When the King is on horseback,
he is sure to be the dirtiest person of the company; and they that make their court best
are such as bespatter him most." If he often
writes so indecently and obscenely as to make
his most characteristic passages quite unquotable, it is not necessarily because he loves
indecency and obscenity for their own sakes,
but the rather because the ugliness of life,
the evil, the defective, and the nauseous, has
come irresistibly to exert a gruesome and
paralytic fascination over his troubled spirit.

So, then, it may have been, with his conduct
toward Stella. That he loved her, no one who
has read the *Journal* can doubt. He is little
short of silly about her. He keeps her letters
under his pillow of nights, and fondles and
caresses and apostrophises them like a smitten
schoolboy :

And, lastly, this morning, Ford sent me two
letters from the coffee-house (where I hardly ever go),
one from the archbishop of Dublin, and t' other

from——. Who do you think t' other was from? I 'll
tell you, because you are friends: why, then, it was,
faith, it was from my own dear little M. D. N. 10.
Oh, but I will not answer it now, no, no-o-o-o-o-h,
I 'll keep it between the two sheets; here it is, just
under. Oh, I lifted up the sheet and saw it there; lie
still, you sha'n't be answered yet, little letter; for I
must go to bed and take care of my head.

But marriage is an act which requires deliberate resolution as well as romantic sentiment,
and that act, with its consequent exposure to
life, it was impossible for him to perform.
Postponed from year to year to an indefinite
to-morrow, it finally, like so many other under-
takings, lost reality for him; it seemed no longer
an affair to be attempted; he had thought it
clean away. For, in spite of all his mutiny and
indiscipline, Swift appears naturally adapted
for the habit of failure. One feels him already
beaten in his sordid London lodgings, writing
that horrible, unconsciously sardonic *Journal
to Stella*, which is superficially but a prosy
chronicle of small economies and petty dis-
comforts and underhand scheming, but in
which the yeasty ferment of the times, the
bickerings of clique and party, the discordant
jangle of motives, social and political, come
somehow, as reflected by his dark, disastrous
humour, to assume a lurid and portentous glare,
like a pandemonium or Sabbath of the Serpents

heaped pell-mell
For devil's roll-call or some feast of Hell.

To repeat the impression of that unexampled
book in a few extracts would be impossible.
The effect is cumulative, and results from the
jostling of innumerable incongruities and discrepancies, from the very welter of discrete
detail which apes afar off and grotesquely life
itself.   But it is easy enough to illustrate the
susceptible spirit which saw life piecemeal
and saw it as a nightmare, the soured sensibility which was alone capable of producing
such a record.   Only compare, for instance,
these two entries for July 25, 1711, and January
3, 1713:

I was this afternoon with Mr. Secretary at his office,
and helped to hinder a man of his pardon, who is
condemned for a rape.   The under secretary was willing
to save him . . . but I told the secretary he could
not pardon him without a favourable report from the
judge; besides, he was a fiddler, and consequently
a rogue, and deserved hanging for something else;
and so he shall swing.   *What!   Must I stand up for
the honour of the fair sex?*
I am just now told that poor, dear Lady Ashburn-
ham, the Duke of Ormond's daughter, died yesterday
at her country house. . . . She was my greatest favourite, and I am in excessive concern for her loss. . . .
Pray condole with me.   'T is extremely moving.   Her
lord's a puppy; and I shall never think it worth my
while to be troubled with him, now he has lost all that
was valuable in his possession ; yet I think he used her

pretty well. *I hate life when I see it exposed to such accidents; and to see so many thousand wretches burdening the earth while such as she die, makes me think God never did intend life for a blessing.*

It is such a revelatory flash as this, amid the gloom of his ordinary temper, which enables us after so many years to catch a glimpse of the heart of the man.

V

To his worldly failure there were, of course, a great many causes contributory. "Great abilities," says Goldsmith, "have always been less serviceable to their possessors than moderate ones." And in a world where moderation and sobriety are looked upon as the safest guarantees of civic virtue, Swift's cleverness was not of a kind to win him any great amount of public confidence. Unable to comprehend the motives by which he was actuated, the public was only bewildered, shocked, and finally antagonised by his sultry and spasmodic brilliancy. Owning no law but their own being, his ideas, conversation, and manners, inasmuch as they were impenetrable, seemed unsettling and incendiary—and the world was right. Swift was in no small degree the dupe of his own cleverness, and was not seldom as guilty of posturing to his own self-esteem as is the charlatan to the approval of others. As to what appears mysterious

in the instrumentality of that defeat, however, for after all the impression with which
one lays down the *Journal* is of amazed conjecture, Swift himself, in several of his papers
on the Tory ministry, throws some light upon
the matter, as far at least as the Queen was
concerned in it. In all probability, she was
already prejudiced against him by reason of
the reckless and irresponsible cleverness of his
Tale of a Tub. Nor can one wonder: to dull,
old dowagers of settled habits, it could not
have been very edifying reading. And from
these papers it further appears that she had
taken on a Tory ministry mainly on account of
her dislike to certain of the Whigs, in particular
to the Duchess of Marlborough, and that the
Tories, with Harley at their head, had hurried
her rather faster than was comfortable along
a road to which circumstances committed her,
though herself a Tory, more irrecoverably than
she liked. Now Swift, as one of the most determined of the party, though not the most
extreme by any means, and as the moulder and
in part director of its policy, could not have
been very agreeable to her in her moderating
inclinations. And it is more than likely,
therefore, that she had a grudge against him
for his very loyalty and activity in behalf of
her own ministry, and took pleasure in grati-
fying it when the matter of his preferment was

laid before her. Such a motive will explain
much that seems at first sight obscure in his
getting nothing better than St. Patrick's, and
that hardly, after his many invaluable services
to the Government. But at the same time,
whatever importance may be allowed to this
and other factors in Swift's disappointment, it
must not be forgotten also that to his worldly
insuccess this trick things had of turning cold in
his hands was probably of no slight significance.

VI

And yet this is the curious thing after all.
In spite of his hopelessness and his final ab-
dication of success, existence never lost its
emotional intensity for him. To judge from
his writings it was indeed no very pleasant picture that life had etched upon his consciousness—a picture in which the ravages of the
corrosive were only too apparent; but it was
at all events a vivid, a poignant one. Nor, what
is more astonishing, had he lost conceit of himself
and his own inviolability. To the world, har-
rowing and garish as it still was, he had risen
superior, in spite of *velléités* and hankerings,
by recognising its fundamental vanity and by
denying it outright to its face. But he never
rose superior to himself in the same fashion; of
his own validity he apparently never had a
saving doubt, and it is just this vulgar sub-

7

mission to the spell of his own being, this
infatuation and pride of self, which accounts
for the acrimony, the virulence, the *sæva
indignatio*, which was the critical trait of his
character.

In his admirable essay on Sterne, Scherer
has pointed out that the foundation of humour
is laid in a cheerful conviction of the utter
nothingness of things human. Now this is
exactly the difference between the mood of
Swift and that of the great English humourists.
Unlike them, he failed, for all his sense of
disenchantment, to observe that he himself
stood in precisely the same case with the rest of
humanity. If they and their earthly concerns
were vanity, then so were he and his. As a
matter of fact, however, his scorn of life was
the result of no philosophical conviction nor
yet of innate grace, but rather of physical and
moral infirmity; it was the temper of defeat.
Along with all his world-weariness and disgust
ran the naïve belief that, however it might
be with others, he himself was fully justified.
He had fought a losing fight. He had lived
in garrets and stinking lodging-houses, doubly
afflicted by poverty and disease, while he was
painfully beating and bullying his way into
prominence. He had been raked up out of
obscurity to serve a government in the menial
capacity of a Grub Street hack, and he had

succeeded in imposing himself upon it and subduing it to a policy of his own. He had been forced to postpone his marriage to the convenience of courtiers and ministers, while he ate the sour bread of dependence, until it had finally grown as unreal and tenuous as a mirage, a thing to dream, not to act on. And in the end he had seen himself, for his pains, relegated to the "mists and fogs of people" whence he had partially emerged, and the cause to which he stood committed, irretrievably ruined. He had failed; he, Jonathan Swift! And as he viewed the disaster, it was Truth and none other that had been discomfited in the person of him, her approved champion. Still taking himself and his own emotions seriously, even solemnly, he had no other means of explaining his overthrow save by assuming the utter depravity of human nature. And the horror of it was, he still cared in spite of his philosophy—indeed, he was almost the sole man of his age who was always desperately and terribly in earnest—else he had not hated and detested as he did.

The chief end I propose to myself in all my labours, so he writes to Pope, is to vex the world rather than divert it, and if I could compass that design without hurting my own person or fortune I would be the most indefatigable writer you have ever seen. I have ever hated all nations, professions, and communities,

he continues. But principally I hate and detest
that animal called man.

It was from this hideous festering of dis-
tempered passions that distilled drop by drop
the slow venom, with whose accumulated
virus he was wont from time to time to slaver
this blistering "carcase of humanity." And
it is for this same cause too that he wants that
sense of human kinship, with its sympathy
for human suffering and its indulgence of
human weakness, which constitutes the other
ingredient of a genuine humour. While the
warp in his nature, his morbid sensitiveness,
and his partiality with respect to his time,
his confusion of prejudice with truth, incapacitate
him equally as a moralist.

VII

In view of these considerations, it will seem
by no means singular that *The Tale of a Tub*
and *Gulliver's Travels*, the two writings most
indicative of his temper, are those of the most
general and enduring literary interest likewise.
Indeed, they are almost the sole pieces by which
his prose is commonly known. For, as a matter of fact, they contain very nearly all of
him, as they also span very nearly his entire
active life. They are both of them brutal
attacks upon that animal called man, but each

from its own point of view and by its own method, the former as he is a religious, the latter as he is a political, animal.

If *The Tale of a Tub* is far and away the best of all Swift's work, as Dr. Johnson used to think, there is good reason for it. The form which he there assumes is, by reason of digression and irrelevancy, thoroughly adapted to the character of his wit and that peculiar reckless cleverness of his, which were both in their typical aspects thoroughly chaotic and fragmentary. The *Tale* is, on the face of it, the sally of a brilliant young man who has just begun to find out a thing or two and is disposed to believe the world rather than himself in a very bad way. As such it is distinguished by an exuberance, an audacity, a headiness which he naturally never again approached. But in spite of its geniality—wherein it is altogether singular among its author's performances— Queen Anne was right. It was a pernicious book, for it attacked, not this or that sect or religion, Dissent or Roman Catholicism, but the whole ground of human nature in which all religion has its root. It already declared the man's first mortifications as *Gulliver's Travels* declared his last.

As a systematic exposure of misanthropy *Gulliver's Travels* has never been equalled. It is not only scathing, it is thorough—it leaves nothing standing, not even the mind that levels. It is so absolutely and relentlessly destructive, that it ends by annihilating itself. In the very contrast between the Liliputians and the Brobdingnags humanity is pitched upon the horns of a merciless dilemma, to show that human character and action are equally ridiculous and contemptible on whatever scale and from whatever point of view they may be conceived; while in further depreciation of human nature Gulliver himself is foisted in between them, for the sake of comparison, like an animated yardstick. On the one hand he is related to the Liliputians as the Brobdingnags to him, and contrariwise, in such a manner as to emphasise the impression which would be produced upon the normal creature by a diminution or magnification of human kind. And, on the other hand, as the representative of humanity he serves himself, in his own person, as the butt of both. But at the same time that mortal pettiness and grandeur are shown to be only a matter of inches after all, it is curious to observe that even Swift has allowed himself to be imposed upon by size, and has let the giants off much more easily than the pygmies.

These are certainly the most ingenious pages that Swift ever wrote, clever as he was, and the most characteristic. They are not altogether pleasant reading, but their acerbity is tem-

pered by the intellectual coolness necessary
to the execution of so ingenious a design. In
this respect they are the best at which to close
withal; for in that final outburst of savagery,
the voyage to the Houyhnhnms, all point, plan,
and even sanity itself are overwhelmed in the
fury of the paroxysm. It were well, then, to
leave him here, baffled, indeed, and desperate,
but not yet distracted, nor attempt to follow
farther into those darker labyrinths where his
cynicism ends, like his own existence, in that
most melancholy and depressing of all spectacles,
the disgrace of reason.

NATURE AND THOMAS HARDY

OF all Mr. Hardy's books, *The Return of the Native* is undoubtedly the one that displays him to the best advantage. *Tess of the D'Urbervilles*, that obsession of hopeless misery, with the grim, sardonic humour licking under its title like a scurrilous tongue— *Tess*, which has long disputed a characteristic pre-eminence—suffers incurably, among other drawbacks, from its incongruous clutter of erotico-psychological sentiment. But in *The Return of the Native* there is nothing to distract from the slow impressive march of tragic circumstance over the sombre rounds and hollows of Egdon Heath; the very nudity of the story only falling in the more harmoniously with the broad and simple outlines of human tragedy. Nor is the reason of this superiority far to seek; for, first of all, before character, before action, Mr. Hardy is the novelist of nature; and gaunt, melancholy, brooding Egdon dominates the novel.

Among the *aperçus* which Stevenson has left us on the subject of his craft, his biographer reports the following:

I know three ways, and three ways only, of writing a story. You may take a plot and fit characters to it, or you may take a character and choose incidents and situations to develop it, or, lastly, . . . you may take a certain atmosphere and get action and person to express and realise it.

A hundred years ago and this last clause would have been scarcely intelligible to the general public; but who is there to-day so insensible to the influences of time and place, "the dreadful hollow behind the little wood," or the shadow "under that grey convent-wall," as not to wish the scene in its typical aspects provided with some complementary attribute of human experience? Such at all events would seem to be the impulse of all Mr. Hardy's work, of *A Laodicean* as well as of *The Woodlanders* —only where he is conspicuously not himself, does it drop into abeyance—the desire to see for once in life man's destiny and circumstances properly suited.

But in this respect, it may be said, he has only continued, like most writers of the nineteenth century, the tradition of Jean Jacques Rousseau. And indeed it is the fashion to talk nowadays as though nature were Rousseau's original discovery and peculiar property; whereas more exactly he was only the first of moderns to see in the spectacle of the outer world a new literary motive and to attempt to raise it, as a literary element, to an equal power with

character and action. The first of moderns I
say, because even then he was after all but a re-
viver of "the vice of the eye," in which the Latin
decadents had been long beforehand with him.
In the introduction of this new element into
literature there is as much to deplore as to
rejoice over; for though the hint was taken
first by the "romanticists" with their innocent
and amusing splashes of "local colour," it
afterwards furnished the "naturalists" with
the suggestion of "environments" that can
by no stretch of language be qualified by either
of these epithets. But, such as it is, this tendency to project the human drama, no longer
upon the background of the universe, but upon
some shallow geographical horizon, has transformed the fortunes of the novel, and too often,
alas! by its predilection for strict localisation
led to a sacrifice of cosmical perspective for the
sake of a very flimsy illusion of reality—a sort
of straitened literary parochialism.

Against all this limitation and restriction Mr.
Hardy has instituted a salutary reaction, even
while appearing, perhaps, to do the contrary—
and that without yielding a single genuine
advantage of those secured by his predecessors.
Though as concerns that narrower conception
of nature of which Jean Jacques may be said
with approximate accuracy to be the originator,
he is necessarily the child of his ancestors, and

more especially of his immediate progenitors,
the "realists"; yet he has given to their notions
an extension of which neither the lugubrious
Senancour nor the methodical Stendhal would
ever have dreamed. Himself he has partly
restored, partly created, an entire country on
the ancient and fabulous territory of Wessex
—like Lyonesse, "a land of old upheaven from
the abyss," "where fragments of forgotten
peoples dwelt"—filling it in with wood and
water, hill and dale, and populating it with
towns and villages of an obsolete and super-
seded life, all in exactest topography and with
a cartographer's minute attention to details.
But with him this varied region, flooded with
sunlight and rejoiced by labour, or lying mysterious under a solitary moon, is no longer mere
scenery, the spectacular decoration of an indifferent comedy, wherein man moves untouched
save for some occasional vaporous sentimentality. On the contrary, it has been pro-
moted to a fatal and grandiose complicity in
human affairs, of a piece with destiny, over-
powering the minds of the actors, tyrannis-
ing over their lives and fortunes, and appearing
in any one locality as but the particular agency
and manifestation of a single consistent, universal power.

Moreover, from this expansion of nature's
rôle there has resulted in the spirit of the

author a conception of destiny as an organic whole, whereby humanity is once more factored with the universe, as at once an integral part and a discordant element—an ideal much larger and more satisfactory in itself and one more agreeable with the modern scientific view than is that which has prevailed for the most part in the literature of the century. And here, if it is well considered, in man's aberration and nature's implacable grudge, that motive of which Clem Yeobright is the type, lies the source of all Mr. Hardy's tragedy and the peculiar grimness with which it is invested. For invariably as the catastrophe falls out in consequence of this dissension, as it were between parent and child, so, no matter how pitiful the human plight in its one aspect, it is always in its other informed with just the touch of malice requisite to suggest some trick of circumstance, played not merely upon man's happiness, but upon his dignity as well. With the one face it appeals to our mortal kinship of infirmity and sorrow, with the other to that passionless company of invisible witnesses, who, like Apollo and Athene aperch on the oak tree, find a careless amusement in the hapless spectacle, ἀνδράσι τερπόμενοι. It is this mixture in his plots of pity and malice, resembling, though with a difference, the profound duplicity of the Greek tragic spirit and the moral

ambiguity of Victor Hugo's "tragic grotesque,"
which is characteristic of Mr. Hardy's manner
of considering his art.

Let us not, however, be thought to underrate
the difference. To our cultivated, or sophisticated, modern sense that tragedy is still lacking
in the upper levels, which like the classic
French fails to recognise the eternal paradox of
life, the irreconcilable discrepancy between
the dignity of man's aspirations and the mean-
ness of his condition, and to turn to the spectators alternate cheeks of pity and mirth. But
in Mr. Hardy, it will have been observed, while
there is abundance of pity, there is no pathos,
because no mirth, no genuine humour. Even
his laughter, that witless cachinnation of
clowns, for which he has been variously ap-
plauded and abused, is dull, brutal, and discordant. The incongruities of our lot he sees
as mockery; and he has chosen to present as
a foil what, instead of relieving the contrast,
serves only to re-enforce it—the dark, irrational
side of nature's dealings with the creature, the
workings of mischance and miscarriage—all, in
short, that literature and art, with their passion
for neatness, order, and clarity, have discarded
as impertinent. Pitiable, indeed, it may be
that the least erected worm should suffer
destruction, pashed by the unwitting foot, it
never guessed of—

Den, wie er sich im Staube nährend lebt,
Des Wandrers Tritt vernichtet und begräbt— .

but at the same time it is just this blind liability to accident which makes the worm a
thing so contemptible. Nor is its plight very
different from those in which Mr. Hardy deals;
while it is for this very purpose, lest this unsettling moral should go unheeded, that he has
appointed to wait upon fatality those sullen
rustic choruses already mentioned, for whom,
insensible to the larger issues of the action,
man is but carrion, and death, in the memorable words of Solomon Longways, is not of
such report as to be respected in the extent
of fourpence.

And yet at the bottom of all this it may be
suspected there lies at least some small kernel
of truth, though it be but a half-truth and no
pleasant subject of contemplation. To the
easy first-class passenger, equipped with all
the desirable virtues and conveniences of earthly
travel, such a view of life may well seem merely
morbid, if not simply false. But who that
has ever wintered in the company of failure
and despair, like Tess on the uplands of Flint-
comb Ash, amid those "strange birds from
beyond the North Pole," "gaunt spectral
creatures with tragical eyes," figuring to the
wrought imagination another disastrous fel-
lowship of invisible unearthly presences—who

that has passed through such experience, as
many there are, will not have brought away
some involuntary sense of unconscious male-
volence and spite, of some nameless perfidy
or perversity at work in his fate, beyond human
control or cognisance, which no mortal prudence can avoid or even foresee?

For indeed, of all his characters, of all this
company of the baffled and discomforted, it is
Mr. Hardy's women who fare the worst. To
them his cosmic irony is most relentless. In
that long gallery of feminine portraits which he
has traced so clearly, there is hardly one that
does not wear, like Lady Constantine and Tess
Durbeyfield, a look of strained and pathetic
amazement at the duplicity and faithlessness
of life. They are quite another creature from
man, at once more elemental and more intricate,
more nearly akin to nature and more susceptible
to her peculiarly feminine teasings. Nor do
they differ less remarkably from others of
their own sex in literature. Dickens's women
are distinguished, in general, for their sensibility, Jane Austen's for their elegance and
decorum, George Meredith's for their sen-
suousness. Mr. Hardy's alone are dominated
almost exclusively by temperament, and temperament, as I conceive it, is nothing more or
less than an excess of the irrational and instinctive. Their motives lie outside the evenly

diffused light of the intelligence in the penumbra and among the shadier recesses of consciousness, whence they rise dizzily like the fumes of wine. Themselves they are usually charming, in their waywardness, like Paula—naturally they are all coquettish, every one of them, but they are incalculable, enigmatic, irresponsible, exasperating. Unintelligible to themselves they are in consequence self-contradictory and inconsistent. Of reasons they know nothing, they seldom understand what they mean or act as they purpose, nor are the consequences ever what they have fancied. They are creatures of illusion, of dream and vision. And the horror is that it is their most natural impulses, the portion of their primitive mother, originally intended for their security and happiness, by which they are finally tricked and confounded, as though nature had turned suicidal or had overreached herself in the violence of her desires.

But this way madness lies. Nor is it fair to insist upon a note which is not Mr. Hardy's highest or clearest, though one, it must be confessed, particularly acceptable to the intellectual confusion and vague emotional ebulliency of the times. But as we often see in literature and art some supreme influence or agency stealing in and overpowering the mind of the maker, just as Flaubert, that victim of

a precise and timid formalism, was once over-
ridden, almost unconsciously it would appear,
by a great moral purpose and produced that
once a masterpiece in *Madame Bovary*, so
when Thomas Hardy is at his best, and frequently, if not in an entire work, yet in long
passages, there we seem to recognise the control
of a broader, serener spirit, wherein these petty
inconsistencies are taken up and reconciled—
something of what we must imagine the spirit
of the perfect whole to be if we could see it
unobscured by our partial thoughts and untroubled by our yeasty passions.

8

HAWTHORNE'S SUPERNATURALISM

IN his essay on Emerson Matthew Arnold makes the following remark about Hawthorne: "Hawthorne's literary talent is of the first order. His subjects are generally not to me subjects of the highest interest; but his literary talent is of the first order, the finest, I think, which America has yet produced,— finer by much than Emerson's." And Edward FitzGerald also writes in one of his letters to much the same effect: "Hawthorne seems to me the most of a Man of Genius America has yet produced in the way of Imagination: yet I have never found an appetite for his Books." There is something a little insular, perhaps, about this attempt to separate the writer's genius from his subject and to interpose a barrier between the appreciation of his manner and that of his matter; but after all Arnold and FitzGerald may be right. It is doubtful, indeed, whether any one but a New Englander, and a New Englander of a certain sort, is so constituted as to relish thoroughly Hawthorne's story—I will not say his subjects, because what Arnold and FitzGerald were unable to enjoy in the case of Hawthorne has as much,

I believe, to do with his treatment of the subject as with that subject itself. But at all events with a public that delights in Mrs. Freeman's thin and washy sketches, and mistakes them for a fair likeness of New England, Hawthorne's case is desperate. In this particular, no doubt, the sense for his subject is lost— or in fact never existed. But as for his literary ability, which Matthew Arnold seems to think an entirely different matter—if his literary ability, by which I suppose is meant his style, is not generally acknowledged as superior to anything of the kind in the country, it is only because of certain prejudices which tend just at this moment to hinder its appreciation.

I suppose that the prevailing conception of prose style at the present day may be fairly called colloquial. That is to say, the standard which is commonly held up before the writer, as the one proper to follow, is that which approaches most closely to the manner of conversation and reproduces to some degree its distinctive tone and character. Write as you talk, we are told, or as nearly so as you can, though it is evident that we can not possibly write as we talk no matter how hard we try. The mistake, however, is in thinking that it is desirable to do so. And it is this unhappy misconception, due to the establishment of a false criterion and aim, which is responsible for a good deal of the slovenliness of contemporary writing, and, what is worse, is fatal to the intelligent enjoyment of a great, if not the better, part of English literature, which was as a matter of fact never written with such a standard or purpose.

Nor is the subject so unimportant as to be dismissed summarily. The two extremes of prose are obviously poetry on the one hand and talk on the other. Between these boundaries extends the region of prose. Good prose is not poetry, nor is it talk. But it ought to be capable of expressing anything between talk and poetry without seeming false or strained or out of place,—just as a well-dressed man will not have to wear his evening clothes in the morning, or a morning suit in the evening, while what he puts on for the day's use will be calculated to fit all occasions without seeming too elaborate for some or too plain for others. So a prose which is too poetic for ordinary uses is a poor prose; and a prose which is too lax for thought is a poor prose likewise. Sometimes there is danger, as with Ruskin, of confounding prose with poetry; and sometimes, as nowadays, of confounding it with talk and of reducing all writing to the level of "journalism." Of course there are some qualities which prose ought to share with speech. It ought to be clear, simple, and flexible. It ought to be capable of conveying a plain business-like meaning, without being inflated or puffed up unseemly. Above all it ought to be thoroughly alive and animated. At the same time it should be more final, definitive, and exact than talk can from its nature expect to be. It ought to be more profound and searching. It ought to be applicable to our graver and more serious uses. And in order to justify its more permanent form—to pay for the pain of writing down and of reading, it should be pure, correct, and stable. That there ought to be a closer correspondence between prose and talk than that which actually exists to-day, I grant. But it is talk which should be elevated, not prose which should be degraded; for as a matter of fact our colloquial medium is growing perceptibly worse from year to year. Slang is increasing; and what is even worse, business and semi-technical cant of all kinds. Idioms are diminishing, and raceless, colourless expressions are constantly substituted, until the basis of our talk, our *Umgangssprache*, is like a bad translation from the Latin, garnished with an occasional sprig of profanity, like a tuft of cowslips in a bog.

Now it is this colloquial decadence of ours, together with the erection of a false standard of prose, which has worked to hinder a just appreciation of Hawthorne's style, and also

perhaps of his unusual literary ability. For
with this conception Hawthorne's style has no
affiliation. It is prose, not poetry; but at the
same time if it is not poetry, neither is it talk
or "journalism." And the distinction is sharp
and unmistakable. Hawthorne wrote without
difficulty apparently, when he wrote. He was
no such filer of phrases as Pater or Flaubert.
But his prose, though not artificial, is yet
artful. It has as much amplitude, fluency, and
rhythm as De Quincey's if of another kind.
It is in the great tradition, the tradition of
Dryden and Burke, though it has naturally
learned something since Dryden—something
too, probably, since Burke. In comparison
with Addison's it is more various and profound,
for Addison himself wrote at the promptings of
a false colloquial taste. But after all what is
most interesting and suggestive about it, is its
chiaroscuro, its penumbra, its suggestiveness.

About the quality itself there is nothing
exceptional nowadays. In a period of slipshod
colloquialism there is nothing so likely to seem
like distinction, to those who are searching for
it, as the finical and the sophisticated. In
this respect Lamb and Pater are nearer the
taste of the time and are profiting by the circumstance. Only in Hawthorne's case the
meaning is of a sort that can be only suggested,
whereas in Pater's at all events it is doubtful

whether there is anything to suggest except
the suggestion. For after all it is necessary
to distinguish between suggestiveness and indefiniteness. It is possible for any one with
little pains to write in such a manner as to
seem suggestive when only indefinite. Obscurity of expression and vagueness of thought
make a pretty fair substitute for profundity.
But in such cases, if the idea were properly
conceived and appropriately indicated, the illusion of depth and significance would vanish.

But with Hawthorne it is quite different.
If on every side beyond the fully illuminated
disc of his meaning there stretches away a
tract of rapidly deepening twilight, filled with
sombre and dubious apprehensions like familiar
things seen under the edge of night, it is due
to the fact that his landscape itself is so overcast
and darkened that its features are indistin-
guishable to the eye and indefinable in words.
Across his consciousness every material object
seems to cast a kind of moral or spiritual
reflection. And just as in a wood the whole
area is so checquered with shade that the real
and the phantasmal are inextricably mingled
and all the air is perplexed with a thousand
flickering illusions as though by a spell or
enchantment, so his vision is blurred and
diffracted by the moral shadow of reality
projected by the light of his own imagination.

And it is this world of impalpable and ghostly
apparitions which he attempts to trace, as well
as the realities which give rise to them. It is
not merely that he recognises the moral influence of material things ; but rather that this
influence becomes itself something extensible
at least, if not actually ponderable, and takes
its place, like a shadow in the landscape. It is
not that his world is a world of effluences and
effects, for so for that matter is every world;
it is rather a haunted world, in which the ghosts
of things walk, not only effectually, but inef-
fectually too. For in the ordinary world the
moral influence of things has no existence
except as they produce a definite effect; whereas
in Hawthorne's world these influences fill the
air like spirits. Take, for instance, the description of Salem in the *Custom House*—"its long
and lazy street, lounging through the whole
length of the peninsula, with Gallows Hill,"
where the witches were hanged and Giles Corey
suffered the *peine forte et dure*, "and New
Guinea at one end and a view of the almshouse
at the other"; "the figure of his grave, bearded,
sabled-cloaked, and steeple-crowned progenitor
—who came so early with his Bible and his
sword"—and notice how these clear substantial figures become gradually attenuated
as they recede, into a "mere sensuous sympathy of dust for dust," while among   them

flickers the bloodless apparition of duty and guilt and crime.

To this equivocal feeling of the illusory and spectral character of material things is due, no doubt, a great part of Hawthorne's "weirdness" or "supernaturalism," as it has been called. But the effect is re-enforced by another kind of transformation or metamorphosis, the reverse of the former. Not only has every ponderable and material body its ghost or spiritual double, but every moral quality too has a kind of spectre or sensuous presentment of its own, by which it seems to prolong or extend itself into the corporeal world along with the substantial objects of sensation which belong there. So evil is no mere abstraction lodging in the brain or immanent in occasional acts; it has also the power to manifest itself directly. Though it may be imperceptible the greater part of the time, there are moments when it gives immediate evidence of its presence. It darkens daylight. In the shape of a physical blemish or deformity it rides its victim; it walks abroad in his person or wears his features like a mask. Or all of a sudden it passes between us and the sun, and we are aware of twilight and a chill. It has no body of its own precisely; but it has a sensible presence, quite distinct from that of the criminal. It is a semi-material something —we know not just what—a half-condensed vapour, an incipient gathering. And so it is that Hawthorne's world becomes wonderfully intricate and suggestive, haunted as it is by the vague shadows of reality and clouded with this nebulous precipitate of vice and virtue. And yet mysterious and disconcerting as it is, with its ambiguous visions and its intricate mazes of light and shade, it is no more unreal than the spirit which it represents—the spirit of New England. And it is equally tragic for the same reason; because of the spell of conscience, which in like manner bewitches and is bewitched by the things of sense.

The consciousness of Hawthorne's New England is anomalous. The Puritans themselves, his ancestors, were dominated by a single idea, an obsession engrossing almost to the point of madness—the idea of duty and guilt, of something owing God and of man's inability to redeem the debt by his own efforts. Under the influence of this idea their life had undergone a momentous transformation. On that precarious strip of coast, so narrow as hardly to afford them footing, between the sea and the wilderness, it had come to seem that life after all was not by any means what it appeared to be, but vaster and more portentous. To all appearance it was with the inclemency of the weather, the hostility of the elements, at most the enmity of the savages that they were contending. In reality all this was but a veil; it was the devil and his ministers, the forces of darkness and evil, the powers of hell that disputed with them for the salvation of their souls. And so to their excited imagination the conflict took on a solemn and grandiose significance. In a struggle of such immortal consequence nothing was too small or remote to remain aloof or unaffected: there were signs in heaven and on earth, omens and portents and forewarnings, earthquake, meteor, and eclipse, or dream and vision. Nor did they feel that they were fighting alone, those watch-worn Pilgrims on the outposts of Christendom; the world of spirits was divided in their quarrel, while reality itself was a mask, which might serve indifferently for the covert of a friend or the ambush of a foe, and where the arch-enemy himself might be found lurking, disguised or in his own person, alone or in council with his agents and witnesses.

And yet this state of mind was hardly superstition. Or if so, it was superstition redeemed by a profound belief in God and in the superlative importance of the individual soul as the capital facts of religion. But when this ancient faith began to fail, as it soon did, when the New Englander had once lost his hold upon the reality of God and the human soul and the seriousness of that great duel of good and evil in which he had felt himself so deeply involved, then indeed his conscience began to sink into error and confusion. The instincts of righteousness and remorse were for a while as strong as ever; but such a feeling, as merely habitual, was bound to wear away. And with increasing distrust of the old realities, the standards by which he had hitherto regulated his conduct, the distinctions of guilt and innocence, the sanctions of duty and responsibility would rapidly grow dim and meaningless. While he might still continue to act and refrain as before, yet his motives and impulses, now that their animating and reasonable principle had lapsed, were doomed to seem inexplicable or even irrational, like faint and incoherent echoes of a long-forgotten tune. In accordance with a prompting from the remoter crannies of the brain or the deeper recesses of memory, he would indeed be able to preserve a kind of superficial consistency; but he would be capable no longer of accounting for himself, and in attempting to do so he might even seem to be actuated by some incalculable instinct or blind fatality. In this general derangement of his moral world former lines of demarcation became gradually blurred or wholly obliterated, until its ill-defined boundaries ceased at last to oppose an obstacle to the intrusion of impertinent and superstitious fancies. And it is this crumbling—or rather this shrinking away—of the old faith from its original metes and bounds, together with the laying bare of that visionary borderland between wind and water, between reality and illusion, which is represented by Hawthorne's dusky chiaroscuro, streaked with the shadows of things imperceptible by direct vision and filled with the air of mysterious and invisible wings.

Characteristically such a confusion of substance and shadow, of the real and the illusory, has something dreamlike about it and is seldom realised with any completeness in a waking state. It is only in a dream that our ideas come before us with sufficient vividness to seem real and that reality dwindles into the semblance of a fume. And it is of this peculiar and significant circumstance that Hawthorne takes advantage to enhance the unearthly and prodigious power of his romance. By adding to the effect of dreamlike ambiguity, already inherent in his mood and manner, a sense of tremendous but paralytic effort, he is able to deepen this elementary impression of dreaming into the very intensity and fascination of nightmare. There is little or none of his best work that does not result in a feeling of impotence and palsy; few or none of his characters that is not hung upon with a misery of irresolution and dismay. It is

in vain that Hester and the Minister would
break the spell that binds them. They can not.
And you anticipate their failure as you over-
hear them in the woods planning drearily to
escape their persecutor. By a sure presenti-
ment you know that when the time comes,
they will never stir a step, just as you foresee
in your nightmares the approach of horror and
the inevitable arrest. And so of Hepzibah
and the luckless Clifford— they too have undertaken to escape—they have even succeeded in
making a start—they seem to have been
travelling endlessly (and was ever a more
phantom journey made by rail than theirs?);
but for all their haste and agitation, when they
are finally brought to a stop, they have gone
but a mile or two. And so it is everywhere—
everywhere the passion and the fever, the
strain and tension; but no successful action,
none of that effort which starts the sluggish
blood and enlarges the cramped and moody
spirit. Motionless, charmed to the ground, sick
with delirious forebodings, the victims await
the catastrophe, which stalks them, in an
agony of helpless consternation. And what is
more, the spasmodic rigidity of their tragedy
answers to the moral truth of their situation.
Like all of Hawthorne's literary devices, it
is a mere symbol. If his characters appear
spellbound and hag-rid, it is because the hor-

ror they would escape is within them and is ineluctable.

And yet in one way is the incubus lightened for the reader into that pacific sense of resignation without which appreciation of tragedy is impossible. In no other particular does Hawthorne differ more widely from the taste of the time than in his exquisite appreciation of tragic beauty. In this respect it can hardly be denied, even by the most ardent apologist of things modern, that the present taste has fallen into lamentable confusion. We are familiar with the manner in which many persons confound moral and physical distress, and are unable to bear mental anxiety without sundry grimaces or contortions, as though they were in bodily agony, or even take to their beds as though in the extremity of health. This is common enough; and it is after the same analogy that we have come to mistake, first the physically, and then the morally, ugly for the tragic, and to believe that whatever is hideous and repulsive in its appearance or its character must necessarily constitute a tragedy. For this idea in its present virulent form Ibsen is chiefly to be thanked. And yet with dramatists like Sophocles and Racine before us it ought to be clear that, whatever else tragedy may be, it can not afford to be ugly. On two occasions Shakespeare himself made a conspicuously

ugly tragedy, *Measure for Measure* and *Troilus
and Cressida*—for however these plays happen
to turn out, they are virtually tragedies. Compared with the other tragedies of Shakespeare,
their anomalousness is curious and striking—
so much so that it has been a kind of puzzle
among critics how Shakespeare came to write
them. He is supposed to have undergone
some serious misfortune, to have been out of
joint with life, to have been suffering from ill
health. But whatever the cause may be, the
result is indisputable; on these occasions at
least Shakespeare wrote ugly. Whether he
actually confounded ugliness with tragedy
or not, these two plays are ugly and that is
why they seem so very modern as to have
won Mr. Bernard Shaw's fastidious approval.
What is amazing about the whole matter,
however, is the circumstance that it should
be perfectly obvious by this time, from the
general attitude of criticism toward them, that
their ugliness is a drawback, not an advantage.
But the mistake has worked so deep, it has
become so firmly embedded in common consciousness and rooted in vulgar speech, where
every shabby bankruptcy and sordid suicide
is a tragedy, that it is not to be easily eradicated
at this late day. But such is not Hawthorne's
idea. He writes tragedy, but his tragedy
is beautiful, not hideous. The *Scarlet Letter*

is in itself a beautiful thing. And it confers,
besides, that benediction which beauty alone
is competent to bestow, whereby what were
otherwise blight and mildew is turned to fairness
and serenity. Nor is this beauty and serenity
in his work as a whole merely external and
superficial. It has its moral counterpart in the
manner in which he himself threads his way,
through this limbo of sense and spirit, amid
these bewildering involutions of light and
darkness, undazzled and untroubled. For
the most remarkable thing about his work is
that he himself is able to keep his head and hold
the balance. He is like a sane man in a mad-
house, who lives among the hallucinations of
the crazed without losing his senses or suffering
his judgment to become warped for a moment.
Amid all the sick fancies of a guilty conscience or
a mind deranged he is never dazed or staggered,
though he walks at times on the dizzy edge of
reason — nor does he allow his reader's eye to
waver or his step to falter. And it is because
he was able to keep his own head and his reader's
on an earth so tremulous and uncertain and in
an atmosphere so fantastic and infected that he
has succeeded with such subjects as he chose
in producing a work which is at once true and
beautiful.

9

DRYDEN AND THE CRITICAL CANONS OF THE EIGHTEENTH CENTURY

I

DRYDEN'S spirit, like that of the whole age which he determined, was largely, as we look at these matters nowadays, a prose spirit. That is, it was marked by common sense or intelligence more strongly than by fancy or imagination. In general terms he may be defined as a man of parts who applied himself to the business of letters. His lack of creative power is very conspicuous. He never in all his plays made a character. His dramas have no illusion. Even their mechanical construction is rather rickety. His themes are usually suggested, and his materials are frequently furnished in part, either by some other writer, as in *Amphitryon*, which is a clever compilation of Molière and Plautus and in some respects better than either, or else by some current truism or commonplace of the day. For this reason he is at his best poetically in translation or in satire. For even in poetry his chief merit is to say things in a downright manner, to hit the nail on the head and hit it hard. This is no despicable quality, to be sure, but it is on the whole a quality more proper to prose than to poetry.

Indeed, in Dryden's conception and practice poetry is very nearly identical with propriety of thought and expression; that is, the thought or the sentiment must be just and the language suitable—clear, discursive, without grammatical violence, ellipses, inversions, and the like. He was not the first, as a matter of fact, to make wit and poetry synonymous; but he was the first to give that definition the support of a systematic criticism and the authority of a powerful example. "Wit," he says, is "a propriety of thoughts and words." And again, "a thing well said is wit in any language." If poetry, therefore, is nothing else than wit, poetry must obviously consist in a propriety of thoughts and words or in saying a thing well. And as this was virtually the idea of poetry that was to obtain for nearly a century and a half in English literature under the general canon of correctness, it would be as well to scrutinise it rather closely.

After all, it can not be denied that there is poetic quality in mere neatness of expression. The saying of a thing simply, clearly, and pointedly is poetic in itself. The French have always recognised such a character in aptness of expression; indeed, rhyme aside, much of

their poetry differs from prose only in being
more nicely expressed. And the French are
right as usual in these matters; for such a
style is essentially organic. It fills the mind
with perfectly clear ideas and images, and dispels
the vague, the obscure, and the nebulous. It
is this property of exquisite aptitude, of saying
a thing plainly and yet fitly, which contributes
to make Keats's *Grecian Urn* what it is—classic
poetry in the noblest sense.

> What little town by river or sea-shore
> Or mountain-built with peaceful citadel,
>   Is emptied of this folk, this pious morn?

Or to take an example from Dryden himself:

> But Shakespeare's magic could not copied be,
> Within that circle none durst walk but he.

Though there is, to be sure, imagination, or at
least fancy, in the figure, it is the propriety
of the expression as a whole which is mainly
responsible for the charm—a propriety which
would not be amiss in prose but would be in its
degree poetic anywhere. Of such bare correctness of expression without imaginative gilding
or alloy it is Pope, however, who is the great
master, as the currency of his phrases testifies.
And remarkably enough, such is the capability
of the process in its perfection, he has succeeded
in imparting to these bald *sententiæ* a kind of
vague emotional thrill, a sort of sentimental

tremolo, as though they were even more than
they are.

> E'en copious Dryden wanted, or forgot,
> The last and greatest art, the art to blot.

This is very little, if at all, better than prose;
and yet how well it apes the sensibility of
poetry!

> The last and greatest art, the art to blot!

It has quite the romantic quaver.

In order to define this idea of propriety a
little more exactly, it might be well to compare,
with such verses as these of Pope's and Dryden's,
a poetry like the Elizabethan, which neither
recognised nor followed any such principle.
In *Troilus and Cressida* Shakespeare has an
admired passage, which begins as follows:

> But value dwells not in particular will;
> It holds his estimate and dignity
> As well wherein 't is precious of itself
> As in the prizer: 't is mad idolatry
> To make the service greater than the God.

Here the purpose is the same as Pope's and
Dryden's—the expression of a general moral
truth. The first four lines lack clearness, but
the figure is admirable and quite in Pope's
and Dryden's way. They might either of them
have been glad to write it, if they could have
done so. But what they never would have

done—they would never have concluded the
passage as Shakespeare does:

> And the will dotes that is attributive
> To what infectiously itself affects
> Without some image of the affected merit.

It was this kind of thing in Shakespeare
and his contemporaries which offended so much
the taste of the succeeding age. And indeed it
is not difficult to conceive that to such an age,
as to Jonson, Shakespeare should seem to have
"wanted art." In his *Defence of the Epilogue*
Dryden remarks:

> Malice and partiality set aside, let any man, who un-
> derstands English, read diligently the works of Shake-
> speare and Fletcher, and I dare undertake, that he will
> find in every page either some solecism of speech, or
> some notorious flaw in sense. . . . Poetry was then,
> if not in its infancy among us, at least not arrived to
> its vigour and maturity: witness the lameness of their
> plots; many of which . . . were made up of some
> ridiculous incoherent story, which in one play many
> times took up the business of an age. I suppose I need
> not name *Pericles, Prince of Tyre*, nor the historical
> plays of Shakespeare: besides many of the rest, as the
> *Winter's Tale, Love's Labour Lost, Measure for Meas-
> ure*, which were either grounded on impossibilities,
> or at least so meanly written, that the comedy
> neither caused your mirth, nor the serious part your
> concernment.

While a little later he speaks of "bombast
speeches of Macbeth," and eventually disposes
of Shakespeare pithily in this fashion:

Shakespeare, who many times has written better than any poet, in any language, is yet so far from writing wit always, or expressing that wit according to the dignity of the subject, that he writes, in many places, below the dullest writer of ours, or any precedent age. Never did any writer precipitate himself from such height of thought to so low expressions, as he often does. He is the very Janus of poets; he wears almost everywhere two faces; and you have scarce begun to admire the one, ere you despise the other.

Now it must be confessed that these extracts do not represent Dryden's best critical tone. They were written in support of certain arrogances to which he had committed himself, when flown with the insolence of success, in an epilogue to the second part of the *Conquest of Granada.* But at the same time they do represent the tendency of his criticism, and what is more important in this connection, the temper of the time in which they were written. And, after all, indiscriminate as the criticism is, it has a kind of general justice. If there is one test by which the work of an artist—for such is the modern equivalent of "wit"—may be known, it is by its evenness, its being all of a piece,—in short, by its propriety. An artist is particularly distinguished by the adaptation of his means to his end. But for the impartial critic to overlook the inequalities—above all, the extravagance and waste—of the Elizabethans, even of Shakespeare himself, is impossible.

The amount of genius that Shakespeare frequently squandered on a play is something appalling, and is quite enough in itself to justify the distinction that Dryden was attempting. For as a matter of fact this distinction between artist and genius, of which so much has been made within our own memory, is quite in the vein of the eighteenth century and was drawn by them before us.   Substantially to the same effect as Dryden, though more temperately, Addison gives to this criticism, in *Spectator* No. 160, what may be called its classical expression:

Among great genius's, those few draw the admiration of the world upon them, and stand up as the prodigies of mankind, who by the mere strength of natural parts, and without any assistance of art or learning, have produced works that were the delight of their own times and the wonder of posterity.   There appears something nobly wild and extravagant in these great genius's that is infinitely more beautiful than all the turn and polishing of what the *French* call a *bel esprit*, by which they would express a genius refined by conversation, reflection, and the reading of the most polite authors. . . .

Many of these great natural genius's that were never disciplined and broken by the rules of art, are to be found among the ancients, and in particular among those of the more eastern parts of the world. . . . At the same time that we allow a greater and more daring genius to the ancients, we must own that the greatest of them very much failed in, or, if you will, that they were much above the nicety and correctness of the moderns. . . .

There is another kind of great genius's which I shall

place in a second class, not as I think them inferior to the first, but only for distinction's sake as they are of a different kind. This second class of great genius's are those that have formed themselves by rules, and submitted the greatness of their natural talents to the corrections and restraints of art. . . .

The genius in both these classes of authors may be equally great, but it shews itself after a different manner. In the first it is like a rich soil in a happy climate, that produces a whole wilderness of noble plants rising in a thousand beautiful landskips without any certain order or regularity. In the other it is the same rich soil under the same happy climate, that has been laid out in walks and parterres, and cut into shape and beauty by the skill of the gardener.

What alone is singular in these statements is Addison's indulgence for the untutored genius, whom he affected rather more than his time, which would hardly have agreed with him in conceding that "both these classes of authors may be equally great." Otherwise the paper is a sufficiently orthodox expression of eighteenth-century opinion.

II

But while it is all very well to propose correctness as an attribute of poetry, there is one obvious difficulty. Without some satisfactory definition and standard of correctness the prescription is useless. In a certain limited sense such a standard is supplied by the ordinances of grammar as well as those of rhyme and metre. But such a standard is not very far-reaching. Although as a matter of fact the writers of the century did not always succeed in satisfying these elementary requirements, they had in mind something more than mere mechanical accuracy. The propriety to which they aspired was elegance rather than exactitude. And of such a quality there is evidently no absolute and indisputable standard. The difficulty is insuperable. Beyond a merely mechanic accomplishment to which any one is capable of attaining by study and industry, excellence is altogether a matter of opinion. For the justification of their poetic performance, therefore, they were obliged, in the last resort, to fall back, like any one else, upon the imponderable arbitrament of taste. But taste, while it can not perhaps be argued, may at least be improved and cultivated like any other faculty. Indeed, as the faculty of literary judgment, it depends very largely for its justice upon a knowledge of literature,—not upon a knowledge of this or that author, or this or that period, or even this or that literature as we seem inclined to believe nowadays, but upon a knowledge of literature as a whole. For Pope and Dryden, however, literature as a whole was represented mainly by Greek and Latin, particularly by the latter; for it is interesting to notice that modern classicism has always been more Latin than Greek. In their time there existed only one great literary achievement in Engish, the Elizabethan, comprising two or three poets of considerable magnitude and no such very great number of lesser lights. A man could read through the bulk of it in a few weeks. But this literature was then in discredit by reason of its final extravagances, to say nothing of certain very conspicuous faults even in its greatest writers, faults to which the succeeding age was particularly sensitive without being particularly sympathetic for its stupendous powers. It lay, as a matter of fact, almost wholly outside the tradition of human culture; its parentage and its congenital temper were decidedly mediæval,[1] while familiarity and distance had as yet failed to soften its numerous asperities. In the eyes of the humanist who was trying conscientiously to form his taste in accordance with the great tradition of human culture, it was thoroughly anomalous and erratic. On the other hand, the literature of contemporary France, which was, besides, in fashion in England for various

---

[1] "I maintain that our national drama was directly evolved from native antecedents, however indirectly modified through the interest which the Renaissance had awakened in the glories of antiquity."—Lewis Campbell: *Tragic Drama in Æschylus, Sophocles, and Shakespeare.*

causes political and social, was just the kind
of literature that would appeal to such a critic.
It was classical; it was conscious of ancient
culture; it was in the great tradition. For
these reasons it was likely to encourage him in
his distaste of Elizabethanism and to draw his
attention to itself and its like away from
the literature of his own country. And he was
the more confirmed in this error because of the
new criticism which was springing up across
the Channel under the hands of Bossu and
Boileau. It has always been one of the fundamental weaknesses of English literature
never to know what it wants. And it is, therefore, not astonishing that a criticism such as
was produced under Louis XIV. should impose
upon a literature like English in making it
conscious of its own rather vague aspirations
and in supplying it with those definite ideas
in which it has always been more or less lacking.
As a practical result, what struck the Englishman as good was that which resembled the
French, while he came to look upon Boileau
and Rapin—"the latter of which," says Dryden,
"is alone sufficient, were all other critics lost,
to teach anew the rules of writing"— very
much as the Renaissance had looked upon
Aristotle.

> Learn Aristotle's rules by rote,
> And at all hazards boldly quote;

Judicious Rymer oft review,
Wise Dennis and profound Bossu.

Under these circumstances it was inevitable
that literature should soon become conventional
and imitative. To be sure, every art without
exception rests finally upon some convention
or other. In this sense, indeed, art is convention.
So in drama the action is supposed transparently
to take place in a kind of three-sided box,
open on the fourth side to the inspection of
men and critics. In the same way the ubiquity
of reader and author is a necessary postulate
of the ordinary novel; while individually the
enjoyment of Browning, for instance, depends
upon the acceptance of a thoroughly arbitrary
dialectic, the so-called dramatic lyric, or lyrical
monologue. For this reason, because of some
similar convention on which his art necessarily
rests, every original genius is likely to strike
the unfamiliar reader as strange and unnatural
at first. At the same time it is necessary to
distinguish. Apparently such a sort of initial
convention is by no means inimical to art. Of
course its general character and its extent
have something to do with the matter. Browning's dramatic lyric is harder to get over than
the ordinary dramatic soliloquy. But on the
contrary nothing could be more conventional
in itself than the English pastoral: and yet
Milton's *Lycidas* is a great poem—perhaps his

finest if not his greatest. If Pope's Pastorals, therefore, are not good poetry, it is not on this account. It is only when a convention is used, not as a foundation for an effect, but as a substitute for the effect itself, that it becomes a blemish and a source of weakness. Even the unities of time and place, which afford some of the purest examples of convention in literature, are capable in the hands of Racine of the happiest results. But when a convention is nothing more than a symbol, standing for a feeling which it is incapable of expressing, then the writer is no longer a poet but an algebraist. In this way arises the poetic formula, the cant or stock phrase or term, the *cliché*, the circumlocution, which are accepted as poetic regardless what significance they actually possess or whether they possess any significance at all. Such in the eighteenth century was the use of words like "Philomela," "nymph," "urn," the personification of abstractions like "Virtue," the retention of antiquated mythological machinery, the arbitrary distinction between the vocabulary of poetry and prose, the deviousness and indirection of paraphrases like the following:

> With slaughtering guns the unwearied fowler roves
> When frosts have whitened all the naked groves;
> Where doves in flocks the leafless trees o'ershade,
> And lonely woodcocks haunt the watery glade,

He lifts the tube, and levels with his eye:
Straight a short thunder breaks the frozen sky:
Oft, as in airy rings they skim the heath,
The clamorous lapwings feel the leaden death.

Even the heroic couplet itself becomes a convention when applied, as it was, to all manner of themes indifferently. By such means as these it is quite possible to write something which will pass for poetry by virtue of rhyme and metre without producing a single genuine poetic effect. And into this sort of thing, it must be confessed that a good deal of the verse of the time resolves.

A little learning is a dangerous thing!
Drink deep, or taste not the Pierian spring.

To say nothing of the *cheville*, "Pierian spring" is pure convention; the remainder of these admired lines are plain prose. The illusion of poetry is produced by the nervous agitation of rhyme and measure.

Naturally the use or abuse of such devices is confined to no one particular literary age or group. This is the way in which Shakespeare himself spells poison.

"The leperous distilment, whose effect
Holds such an enmity with blood of man
That swift as quicksilver it courses through
The natural gates and alleys of the body,
And with a sudden vigour it doth posset
And curd, like eager droppings into milk,
The thin and wholesome blood."

And even to-day, when we are still suffocating with righteous indignation against Pope, there is supposed to be some particular virtue resident in words like "fulfil"—

> fulfilled of precious spice,

and phrasing like

> His eyes were strange and glad and perilous.

Such vices are usually indicative of second-hand inspiration and literary decline. But even so, although they were no more an essential part of the poetic programme of the eighteenth century than they are of ours, yet there has probably never been another school so liable to such errors by the very nature of its poetical postulates and theory.

And the same general remark is true also with regard to its character for imitation. The danger of imitation is one that besets every literary movement. After the peculiar conception of art which inspires a particular movement has been thoroughly worked out and brought to all possible perfection, there is nothing left save to repeat the formula indefinitely or else to find a new idea and strike out a new line of development. That is the eternal difficulty of art—its impermanence. After an innovator like Dryden there is still much to be done in carrying out the ideas which he has succeeded in realising—perhaps recognising—only partially.

After Pope, however, there is nothing for it
except imitation or a new school. But this
imitation, which is incidental to the culmination
of every art, was rather essential to that of the
eighteenth century on account of the character
of its fundamental tenets—the dogma of the
distinction and fixity of *genres* and the dogma
of absolute and permanent literary perfection,
survivals both of them of Renaissance criticism,
for which we have not yet entirely rid ourselves
of a certain amount of traditional and superstitious veneration. In accordance with such
a faith every after-poet was necessarily a copyist.
He could not alter, or he deformed, the *genre;*
improvement and modification were alike impossible. At most he could only adapt. Theo-
retically, therefore, the whole classic movement
was an imitation. Practically, however, the
English did add something of their own both
to the forms and the ideas which they took
from others. Their temper was their own, and
so were the conditions which their adaptations
had to meet, so that their work has a distinctive
tang after all. Their drama, for instance,
cramped as it is, is still broader, freer, and bolder
than the French, though it is looser, more
licentious, and inchoate too. Like most bor-
rowers they were as likely as not to acquire
their neighbours' vices without correcting their
own. Even their originality is a result of their

defects—or at least of their limitations—
domestic and foreign, and belongs to their prose
rather than to their poetry. In prose, as it
happened, they were innovators. But on the
whole, consonant as their literary theory was
with their mood at the time, they got it,
as a conscious possession, from others. Un-
prompted from without they would probably
have never come to literary consciousness at
all. At the same time the prompting was
opportune and agreeable. In giving shape and
solidity to what was floating vaguely in their
own minds, it was just the kind of thing to
which they were inclined to listen. There is a
curious assumption which has worked its
way pretty generally into modern criticism,
as though the school of Dryden and Pope had
been wickedly seduced from their proper alle-
giance to the Elizabethans by the perfidious mis-
representations of French critics. But as a matter
of fact it was the English themselves who helped
to raise the prejudice and who threw themselves
into the embraces of the stranger because they
did not care for Shakespeare and his colleagues.
The truth is that Elizabethanism was on the
lees. Its genius had evaporated, leaving its
extravagance exposed and impudent. And it
was to the example of French literature and the
instruction of French criticism that the new
age turned for confirmation and support in a

reaction whose direction had been fatally
determined in that particular sense by internal
conditions.

At the same time it must not be forgotten
that they borrowed on principle. Only in this
way can the extent and barefacedness of their
pilferings be understood or accounted for. It
was virtuous to imitate, if not an impeccable
antiquity, then those who had appropriated
such an antiquity. And in accordance with the
same logic by which they had acquired their
ideas, they acquired their materials also. What
they did not observe was that in doing so they
were prolonging, curiously enough, the Elizabethan decadence. It is Fletcher whose name
is always in their mouths and in whose footsteps
they follow until they finally discover Corneille
and Bossu. It may be that their invention was
feeble; it was bound to seem so at all events.
Even Dryden appears at his best in set exercises,
in translation, or in other instances where
his theme is given him. "In general," he
declares, "the employment of a poet is like
that of a curious gunsmith, or watchmaker;
the iron or silver is not his own; but they are the
least part of that which gives the value: the
price lies wholly in the workmanship." And
he boldly shoulders the consequences of the
theory. His best drama is probably *All for
Love*, which is made over from Shakespeare's

Antony and Cleopatra. With D'Avenant's assistance he applied the same process to the *Tempest;* and with Lee's, to the *Œdipus*, though with less success in both cases. By himself he "accommodated" *Troilus and Cressida*, for the sake of removing "that heap of rubbish under which many excellent thoughts lay wholly buried"; and turned Molière's *l'Etourdi* into *Sir Martin Mar-all.* But his most extraordinary feat was his dramatisation of Milton's *Paradise Lost* in heroic couplets under the title of *The State of Innocence and the Fall of Man.* To this transmogrification he succeeded in obtaining Milton's consent; but the production was never staged. In addition to all such rehabilitations he translated liberally from Latin, Greek, Italian —and Chaucer. Nor was the case of Pope very different. He inspires himself with Horace and Boileau. A good deal of his best work is a *pastische* of Latin satire. In the *Essay on Man* he versifies ideas which were furnished him immediately by Bolingbroke and whose significance he did not clearly understand, while most of his pieces seem the result of successive sketches— a various patchwork or mosaic which precludes the notion of original projection. But why multiply examples? When such are the leaders of an age, what can be expected of their followers—of the Crowns and Ravenscrofts, the Gays and Priors? Let Addison answer for them all.

When I have finished any of my speculations, it is
my method to consider which of the ancient authors
have touched upon the subject that I treat of. By
this means I meet with some celebrated thought upon
it, or some similitude for the illustration of my subject.

In short, the consciousness of the age was what
we should now call "literary." It was haunted
by the memory of books, saturated with remi-
niscences, distracted by the thought of tradition and authority, of rules and models. And
even in as far as it succeeded in expressing its
own temper, the terms in which it did so were
largely second-hand and foreign.

III

But in spite of these sources of weakness and
the incidental errors to which they gave rise,
or rather on account of the spirit which was
liable to such weaknesses—the spirit of order,
sobriety, and clearness—it is to this movement
that English is indebted for a genuine prose. Of
these errors the general character is sufficiently
obvious. In their respect for correctness and
the authority which was supposed to be its sole
warrant, the promoters of the movement were
apt to become over-anxious and timid; attempting to avoid obscurity and confusion they would
run as likely as not into the opposite extreme
of obviousness and commonplace; against shallowness and triviality their admiration for pre-

cision and lucidity furnished little or no protection; while in their aspiration for elegance and
ease they were in danger of completing the mis-
chief by polishing all the freshness and animation
out of their work and leaving it insipid and lifeless.   And yet, however unfortunate these vices,
they were not incompatible with the idea of
prose, as were the very virtues of Elizabethanism.   In justice to their successors it is only
fair to remember that the Elizabethans did
not do everything.   Dramatic poetry and the
shorter, more spontaneous variety of lyric they
had brought to an advanced state of perfection.
Outside of this field, however, they had done
little or nothing.   When Ben Jonson attempts
to write couplets, the result is lamentable;
nor are Shakespeare's own much to brag of,
while with prose they had failed signally.   As
far as their prose had any literary significance
at all, it was nothing more or less than deversi-
fied poetry.   When Thomas Browne wrote
his *Religio Medici*, it was apparently all he
could do to refrain from dropping into verse.
Rhythm, cadence, the very movement of the
language, the mood itself are all poetical—
nothing is wanting but metre, and that hardly.
Even Milton, who has a prose purpose, is unable
to strike the prose note and hold it.   Naturally
there are one or two exceptions.   Thomas Fuller
stumbles upon the right track occasionally.

Above all, Cowley's essays are thoroughly admirable, though they had no following at the time and have won no appreciation since, probably because his factitious splendour as a poet has eclipsed his genuine merits as a writer of prose. On the whole, however, the predecessors of Dryden lacked a plain prose intention—the sense for a sober, every-day meaning and for a vehicle for its conveyance. And while the need for such a vehicle must have been felt and felt sorely, they seem to have been incapable of distinguishing between the characteristic moods of prose and poetry. With the poetical qualities of feeling, imagination, and temperament they were generously endowed; of the prose qualities of measure, restraint, precision, and reason they were well-nigh destitute.

Nor is the lustre of the achievement diminished by the circumstance that the distinction as once established has been again obliterated. In spite of the havoc and confusion wrought by De Quincey, Ruskin, and Pater, it is the tradition of Addison and Swift which represents, for all their faults, the *genre tranché*, the English prose idea in its integrity. Of this prose, it should be borne in mind, Dryden, however high his deserts, was but the originator. With him prose was very largely a means to an end, a matter of business rather than of literature, an instrument for the production of prefaces, dedications, manifestoes, and proclamations of one sort and another incidental to the actual practice of his art in poetry and drama. Had the case been otherwise, had he failed to divest himself of his literary pretension, to begin with, it is doubtful whether his experiments would have turned out very much better than those of his predecessors. As a consequence of his literary *insouciance*, however, his style is naturally very uneven and irregular. He has an official statement to make, a matter of professional business to transact; and he is by no means finical about the manner in which he expresses himself. Nor is it quite fair to expect of him as a beginner that he should thoroughly explore the path upon which he was the first to stumble, or should himself bring his own invention to perfection. For that we must look to a later period, to the period of Swift and Addison.

In the interval, however, though the general conception remains unchanged, the accidental standards have suffered a gradual transformation. Of Dryden's prose the main characteristic is energy. Even at its best it has something of the clumsiness of a bludgeon. In spite of his artlessness and informality it is evident that he still feels written language as something quite different from spoken. By Addison's time, however, conversation has come to be the general standard of prose. For the change the coffee houses, with their concourse of "wits" and their interminable talk, are in part responsible; but more so, probably, the new comedy, the "comedy of manners," whose dialogue was in reality the only model in existence of a prose at once practicable and literary. But however it happened, the ideals of prose and conversation had become very nearly identical in the minds of Addison and his contemporaries. Not that they wrote exactly as they talked; that was of course impossible. But they aimed to write as they would have liked to talk if they had been able. They tend constantly to obliterate the distinction between the two standards, the literary and the colloquial. Fluency, ease, discursiveness become the *desiderata*. Profundity comes to seem pretentious, even a little absurd. Seriousness itself is in rather bad taste. It is desirable to be suave, agreeable, perspicuous at any price. Such is the false ideal which is mainly accountable for Addison's shallowness and superficiality, for the peculiar listlessness and dejection which are the characteristic effects of his style. His prose is all very pretty, no doubt. One quality of the rarest in English it does at least possess—urbanity. But in the long run it is extremely insipid and cloying.

For this reason Swift is to be preferred in many respects to Addison. At his best Swift is neither commonplace nor yet difficult. He is seldom

urbane, often very coarse, sometimes very vulgar, occasionally extravagant and fantastical
in his pursuit of humour.   Above all, he wants
balance.   With his age and himself he is thoroughly out of tune,—capricious, self-willed, and
arrogant.   And from his infirmity of temper
his style suffers sadly; for as a general thing
prose is much more closely affiliated than poetry
with character.   Vivacity counts for a good
deal more in poetry than in prose: about a poetic
style there is always something exceptional and
factitious; while prose, on the contrary, requires
a sustained and regular effort.   And yet with
all these drawbacks Swift's prose is at its best
the best of the period.

Nevertheless, there is this to be said for Addison.   It is neither possible nor desirable, perhaps, that a moralist's ideas should be very new
or startling; for his general principles, if not
obvious on statement, will carry little or no
conviction.   His originality will consist in
the striking and suggestive application of a
small number of universally accepted or acceptable truths.   Addison, therefore, is not to be
blamed because his ideas are few and familiar.
He is to be blamed only as his development of
such ideas is otiose or insignificant.   When he
endeavours, for instance, "to shew how those
parts of life which are exercised in study, reading, and the pursuits of knowledge, are long but

not tedious, and by that means discover a
method of lengthening our lives and at the same
time of turning all the parts of them to our advantage," he starts an interesting and fruitful
topic of speculation; while in such illustrations
of ordinary moral commonplace as are associa-
ated with the names of the *Spectator* and *Sir
Roger de Coverley*, he has laid literature under
lasting obligation. But when he spends several
pages to prove that a man's acts are not always
a sure guide to his character, then he wastes his
own time and abuses his reader's patience.

Half a century later, however, the unrelieved
triteness into which this conversational prose
finally ran, had become thoroughly irksome.
By Johnson's day there is a vague suspicion that
literature ought, not only to differ from talk,
but also to go deeper than talk usually can go.
Johnson himself, harking back instinctively to
Sir Thomas Browne, attempts more or less
deliberately to restore to prose certain of its lost
powers by the use of a highly Latinised diction
and a highly complicated sentence-structure.
In this way he does succeed occasionally in
scooping up rather more bottom, and at all
events he is always sure of roiling the waters
into a passable imitation of profundity. But
however clumsy his means, such is undoubtedly
the significance of his style. And of this change
of opinion nothing can be more indicative than

the contrast between his spoken and written language, which is so striking as fairly to justify Macaulay's epigram that when he wrote he did his sentences out of English into Johnsonese. Invariably direct, idiomatic, and incisive in his talk, in his writing he was equally as involved, ponderous, and roundabout. "When we were taken upstairs," he writes to Mrs. Thrale in one of his letters from the Hebrides, "a dirty fellow bounced out of the bed in which one of us was to lie." In his published account of the incident as it appears in the *Journey to the Hebrides* the sentence has been transmuted thus: "Out of one of the beds, on which we were to repose, started up at our entrance, a man black as a Cyclops from the forge." Of Buckingham's *Rehearsal* he is said to have remarked that it had not wit enough to keep it sweet, adding after a moment, "It has not vitality enough to preserve it from putrefaction."

In spite of the perplexity which this procedure of his seems to have caused the critics, who are never weary of protesting their amazement that the same man should talk so straight and write so crooked and of fabricating ingenious explanations to account for the mystery, it is perfectly evident what Johnson was driving at. It is perfectly evident in the first place that he drew a very sharp distinction between talk and literary prose. And it is equally

evident that he was doing his best to raise that
prose from the colloquialism into which it had
fallen, and to give it another excellence than
that of conversation.   In this purpose of enlarging and deepening the content of English
prose he was frequently unsuccessful; occasionally, however, he does succeed—at least nearly
enough to indicate his intention and suggest the
idea to others.   And as his contribution to English prose has never been accurately defined or
liberally appreciated, it may be worth while to
quote at length a significant passage.   He is
commenting on the remark attributed to Milton
that "his vein never happily flowed but from
the autumnal equinox to the vernal."

This dependence of the soul upon the seasons, those
temporary and periodical ebbs and flows of intellect,
may, I suppose, justly be derided as the fumes of vain
imagination. *Sapiens dominabitur astris*.   The author
that thinks himself weather-bound will find, with a
little help from hellebore, that he is only idle or exhausted.   But while this notion has possession of the
head, it produces the inability which it supposes.   Our
powers owe much of their energy to our hopes; *pos-
sunt quia videntur*.   When success seems attainable,
diligence is enforced; but when it is admitted that the
faculties are suppressed by a cross wind, or a cloudy sky,
the day is given up without resistance; for who can
contend with the course of nature?

From such prepossessions Milton seems not to have
been free.   There prevailed in his time an opinion that
the world was in its decay, and that we have had
the misfortune to be produced in the decrepitude of

Nature.   It was suspected that the whole creation languished, that neither trees nor animals had the height or bulk of their predecessors, and that everything was daily sinking by gradual diminution.   Milton appears to suspect that souls partake of the general degeneracy, and is not without some fear that his book is written in *an age too late* for heroic poesy.

Another opinion wanders about the world, and sometimes finds reception among wise men; an opinion that restrains the operations of the mind to particular regions, and supposes that a luckless mortal may be born in a degree of latitude too high or too low for wisdom or wit.   From this fancy, wild as it is, he had not cleared his head, when he feared lest the *climate* of his country might be *too cold* for flights of imagination.

Into a mind already occupied by such fancies, another not more reasonable might easily find its way. He that could fear lest his genius had fallen upon too old a world, or too chill a climate, might consistently magnify to himself the influence of the seasons, and believe his faculties to be vigorous only half the year.

His submission to the seasons was at least more reasonable than his dread of decaying Nature, or a frigid zone; for general causes must operate uniformly in a general abatement of mental power; if less could be performed by the writer, less likewise would content the judges of his work.   Among this lagging race of frosty grovellers he might still have risen into eminence by producing something which *they should not willingly let die*.   However inferior to the heroes that were born in better ages, he might still be great among his contemporaries, with the hope of growing every day greater in the dwindle of posterity.   He might still be the giant of the pigmies, the one-eyed monarch of the blind.

The passage, though in a sense exceptional,

is indicative. It shows Johnson's aim, if not his average achievement. What is extraordinary about it is its chiaroscura, its evident effort to suggest something more than can be defined and yet to do so without imperilling the common sense and sanity proper to prose. Such echoes as these had not been wakened in English for many a day. "These bursts of light and involutions of darkness; these transient and involuntary excursions and retrocessions of invention"—it is in such terms that he speaks a little later of the intermittent efforts of genius; and the phrasing is presageful of the new order—an order, however, which it was reserved for Burke to establish. And here at last we have the high-water mark of English prose—a prose which is distinct from talk and deeper without being turgid or cumbersome, which is dignified and imposing, and yet flexible and business-like. Faults it has, for English prose always has had and always will have great faults. It is bound to be in extremes of one kind or another; if it is not lacking in spirit, it is subject to *coups de tête*. But at its best Burke's is perhaps the best on the whole that we have in the way of prose as an instrument of thought. It unites the greatest number of powers with the smallest number of failings of any prose in the language. I do not mean to say that Addison's and Swift's are not sometimes better in some respects; but neither of them has the compass of Burke's. Sir Thomas Browne's and De Quincey's and Ruskin's may have pushed farther in some directions, but they have done so at the expense of their integrity. In short, while this or that author may have excelled or surpassed Burke, acting independently or upon his suggestion, yet he does at least represent in himself the most that prose can do and still remain prose.

IV

While the canon of propriety and correctness, therefore, is not necessarily inimical to poetry, the danger for Dryden and his successors evidently lay in the extremity to which they were likely to push it in the heat of their resentment against what they regarded as the barbaric extravagances of their predecessors. At the same time, however, that, in insisting upon the salutary virtues of moderation and restraint, they would seem to be in equal danger with romanticism of confounding poetry and prose and of reducing all literature, though inversely, to a single standard, the standard of prose; yet as a matter of fact, like every classical coterie, they made a very sharp distinction, perhaps the sharpest that has ever been made in English, between the two—or at least between prose and verse. To be sure, the *differentia* are not very

easy to define and are mostly formal. But it
seems clear enough at all events that Dryden
still considered poetry to be the more elevated,
though he may not have understood very well
what poetic elevation really is. Of blank verse
he complains that it is less suitable than rhyme
for tragedy because it is not sufficiently elevated.
"Blank verse is acknowledged to be too low for
a poem, nay more for a paper of verses; but if too
low for an ordinary sonnet, how much more for
tragedy . . . ?" Poetic elevation, then, would
seem to depend upon rhyme. Poetry, at all
events poetry of a high order, must rhyme. And
in conformity with this notion he falls into
the habit of calling blank verse prose, "blank
verse being," he says "but measured prose."
"Whether Heroic Verse ought to be admitted
into serious plays, is not now to be disputed.
. . . All the arguments which are formed
against it, can amount to no more than this,
that it is not so near conversation as *prose*, and
therefore not so natural."

Such was the fatal misconception which
resulted in well-nigh shelving blank verse completely for a century and in confirming the
general prejudice against Shakespeare as a poet
and artist. For if blank verse is no better than
prose, what becomes of the poetic pretensions
of those who wrote it? And yet, fatuous as the
mistake seems to us, it must be remembered

in Dryden's excuse, and in that of his contemporaries, that such was the pass to which blank verse had been brought by this time as to make it almost impossible to form a just conception of the measure either in itself or as a basis for an estimate of Shakespeare's versification. For the time being romanticism was thoroughly played out. And although French influence had a good deal to do with the erection of rhyme into an invariable poetic standard, as it had with all the literary positions occupied by English classicism, yet more important by all odds than any foreign influence was the spirit of opposition that had finally been engendered by the extremity of the age preceding.

Under these circumstances the heroic couplet became inevitable, not merely by reason of the encouragement afforded by the French alexandrine, but even more by the very nature of the case. It combined the national line with rhyme; it was the only form of rhyme capable of anything like general application; and especially it suited the kind of subject and effect acceptable to the new poetry. Two lines of ample extent, set off one against the other and yet forming a distinct system in themselves, compact, regular, and symmetrical, capable of antithesis or parallelism—what better vehicle could be imagined for the conveyance of that glorified commonsense on which the age prided itself? Nor are its possibilities exhausted by the expression of clear ideas. To do it better justice it is necessary only to think of Professor Santayana's comparison of a Greek colonnade; to recall Thackeray's admiration for the close of the *Dunciad*—lines, he declares, in which Pope "shows himself the equal of all poets of all times"; and to remember that Tennyson had at least one passage of Crabbe by heart:

> Early he rose and looked with many a sigh
> On the red light that filled the eastern sky;
> Oft had he stood before alert and gay,
> To hail the glories of the new-born day:
> But now dejected, languid, listless, low,
> He saw the wind upon the water blow,
> And the cold stream curl'd onward as the gale
> From the pine-hill blew harshly down the dale;
> On the right side the youth a wood survey'd,
> With all its dark intensity of shade;
> Where the rough wind alone was heard to move,
> In this, the pause of nature and of love,
> When now the young are reared, and when the old,
> Lost to the tie, grow negligent and cold—
> Far to the left he saw the haunts of men,
> Half-hid in mist, that hung upon the fen;
> Before him swallows, gathering for the sea,
> Took their short flights and gathered on the lea;
> And near the bean-sheaf stood, the harvest done,
> And slowly blackened in the sickly sun.

Unfortunately, however, in despite of authority or tradition, its defects are not only obvious but are so obnoxious to our present prejudices

as to have quite blinded us to its equally obvious
merits. It is monotonous, formal, cut and dried,
lifeless, wooden, inflexible. Some wit has lik-
ened it to the couple of dry sticks which a savage
rubs together in hopes of striking a spark. Even
its clarity has come to be a reproach. But none
the less has our scorn of it cost us a literary *genre*
which we can hardly afford to be without. To
the expression of a certain kind of wisdom—not
altogether unworldly, perhaps, and yet by no
means destitute of seriousness and elevation—
a composition of pathos, satire, and humour, of
the pity and the folly of life, in varying proportions, there is no verse so well adapted. That
such a poetry—a poetry of which Pope's *Epistle
to Dr. Arbuthnot* is an excellent example—no
longer exists in English is probably due to the
gradual deformation of the couplet. For just
as Dryden misjudged and despised blank verse
because he knew it as a living species only in a
corrupt and degraded shape, so we, as though
in revenge, have mutilated the couplet until its
powers are no longer recognisable, and biting
off our nose to spite our face, have lost the use
of one at least of our literary senses.

Immersed

In thought so deeply, Father?   Sad, perhaps?
For whose sake, hers or mine or his who wraps
—Stih plain I seem to see!—about his head
The idle cloak,—about his heart (instead

Of cuirass) some fond hope he may elude,
My vengeance in the cloister's solitude?
Hardly I think!   As little helped his brow
The cloak then, Father—as your grate helps now!

This is what the heroic couplet has become in our hands.   It is nothing but blank verse tagged with rhyme—and poor blank verse at that—a nondescript such as Jonson and Donne wrote, not a distinct measure with its own character and its proper beauty, such as Pope finally brought to perfection.   It is the primitive and undifferentiated rudiment from which Dryden began, and as such it ignores and confounds the labour and the achievement of a century.   What wonder that the *genre* for which the couplet was particularly suited should have perished and that poetical satire is dead!   The astonishing thing is that now, when men's minds are at last beginning to change, none of our teeming young poets has as yet perceived the possibility of a revival.

But to return to Dryden's conception of poetic excellence.   In addition to rhyme poetry must possess mellifluousness.   Of all things harshness was most to be reprehended as "Gothic" and barbaric.   "Well placing of words for the sweetness of pronunciation," says Dryden, "was not known until Mr. Waller introduced it."   His own translation of the first line of the *Iliad* likewise he modestly commends for its smoothness, though it is composed of mono-syllables,

Arms, and the man I sing, who forced by fate.

Without stopping to discuss the quality of this particular verse, we may venture to admit the general contention that poetry ought to be well sounding and that the words ought to be disposed to help the pronunciation and to tickle the ear without injuring the sense, in their natural order withal, and in accordance with the idiom of the language, without violation of grammar or logic.   But here it is necessary to make a distinction.   The mellifluousness of Dryden and his followers is not to be confounded in the modern manner with melodiousness.   There are two kinds of confusion to which modern poetry is particularly liable.   On the one hand, it is inclined to imitate the illusion of painting by a systematic evocation of visual detail, "vizualisation," so as to produce a sort of verbal or linguistic mirage; on the other hand, that of music by a style of composition in which words are treated rather as notes than ideas.[1]   But for that mellifluousness, that charm of sound proper to language as such, irrespective of purely metrical and musical effects, it has small concern. Not infrequently, indeed, where the musical

[1] *Cf.* R. L. Stevenson, *Style in Literature: Its Technical Elements*, the latter half.

prepossession is absent, it seems perfectly insensible to cacophony and verbal disorders of every sort, if it does not actually affect them as picturesque or forcible or onomatopœic in some sense or other.

> Poor vaunt of life indeed,
> Were man but formed to feed
> On joy, to solely seek and find and feast;
> Such feasting ended, then
> As sure an end to men;
> Irks care the crop-fed bird? Frets doubt the maw-
> crammed beast?

That is a clatter, a hubbub, a linguistic chaos. In the face of such licentiousness one is bound to believe that art ought to be a little artificial, at all events very artful. And it is upon the legitimate euphony of speech, in contrast with this sort of thing, and not upon musical mimicry, which Dryden insists. Of this property of words he seems, as a matter of fact, to have had some small sense, though to what may be called the intrinsic charm of their associations he is much less responsive. "There is a beauty of sound," he says, "in some Latin words, which is wholly lost in any modern language"; and he instances "that *mollis amaracus*, on which Venus lays Cupid in the first *Æneid*. If I should translate it sweet marjoram, as the word signifies, the reader would think I had mistaken Vergil; for

these village words, as I may call them, give us
a mean idea of the thing."

In the face of this observation it is amusing to
find Malone in his edition of Dryden taking the
poet to task for just such homely and "village"
words as the critic has here been condemning.

> He wrote in general with as much spirit as any man,
> and in this work, the translation of Vergil, was pressed
> by other causes to write with yet more rapidity than
> usual.   This must have occasioned several negligences,
> and among the rest some low expressions and mean
> lines, sometimes very unworthy of the subject he is
> treating.   Hence he speaks of Bacchus's honest face
> and of the jolly autumn.   It is hence that he calls Juno
> the buxom bride of Jupiter, and Cybele the grandam
> goddess.   It is thus that he speaks of Juno's sailing
> on the winds and Apollo's bestriding the clouds."

This is turning the tables with a vengeance
and out-centuring the century.   But the fact
is that Dryden had a natural vivacity and exuberance which sometimes carried him beyond
his own theories and put his criticism hard to it
to follow.   For it must be remembered that
Dryden had this trait in common with Lessing
and other critics who have been writers as well:
he criticises from the craftsman's point of view.
His criticism is largely a criticism of method.
This peculiarity makes it very instructive with
regard to the ideas of the time.   But naturally
enough under the circumstances it is blind to
everything outside his own performance, the

kind of thing that he was trying to accomplish
himself at the moment. In short, he seldom
perceives a critical position before he has taken
it up poetically. In a sense he furnishes his own
data just as he illustrates his own dicta; and all
his criticism is self-criticism. Hence his art
and his appreciation develop hand in hand.
And as he has no hesitation in recording his opinions as fast as they change, his constant development gives his criticism an appearance of
inconsistency which is occasionally disconcerting. A poet is expected to grow; he is indulged
in half a dozen manners, if necessary. But,
unreasonably enough, the critic is expected to
form his conclusions once for all and stick to
them inflexibly. And yet one of the most praise-
worthy, as surprising, things in Dryden's
criticism is just this capacity for growth. There
is hardly a matter of taste touched in his earlier
work with regard to which he has not changed
his mind sooner or later for the better, for with
regard to his fundamental principles he remains
pretty nearly fixed. He comes to have a very
much higher opinion of Shakespeare, without
relinquishing the original grounds on which he
criticised him at first. He reverses his opinion
with respect to the relative dramatic merits of
the couplet and blank verse without altering his
general theory of dramatic poetry, as I shall try
to show a little later. And it is very probable

that if he had bethought himself he would finally have passed quite another judgment upon "sweet marjoram" and such like "village words" and one more in accord with his own example. But however this may be, it is precisely the fixity of his fundamental principles and the flexibility of his application which constitute his merit as a critic.

V

It is obvious from these instances that the school of Dryden and his successors was likely to have scant patience with enthusiasm of any sort. Even in the mouth of Addison, the most liberal, the most open to alien ideas of them all, it is a term of reproach, synonymous with bad taste, license, and extravagance. From their particular point of view poetry was a judicious exercise of the intelligence, not a *rausch* or an intoxication. Substantially it consisted in a neat and epigrammatic way of expressing general truth. And its practitioners probably thought quite as well of their *sententiæ* as we do of our "purple patches," and very likely with quite as good reason. In fact, it is difficult to see what other advantage than its modishness Tennyson's *In Memoriam* possesses over Pope's *Essay on Man*, in the eyes of whose contemporaries "reason alone is sufficient to govern a rational creature." In his life of Milton Johnson

defines poetry as "the art of uniting pleasure
with truth by calling imagination to the aid of
reason." And in the same strain he explains
genius as "a mind of large general powers acci-
dentally determined to some particular direction." While to like effect Addison laments
"the unhappy force of an imagination unguided
by the check [*sic*] of reason and judgment." And
slight as it is at best, even this apparent conces-
sion to imagination is merely nominal, for it
must not be forgotten that in the interval the
significance of the word has suffered something
of a change. In the intention of the eighteenth
century, imagination was more nearly identical
with what we now think of—if we ever think
of it at all—as the constructive faculty, than
with that state of ecstatic excitement which
is usually signified by the word at present.
Whereas the art of writing has finally come of
modern times to be associated with the pictorial
and the musical arts, it was in those days regarded rather as plastic or structural, while the
analogies by which it was illustrated were drawn
largely from architecture. Agreeably with this
view the literary or poetic imagination was considered to consist mainly in the ability to plan,
to conceive a whole through the disposition of
a number of parts. But this faculty is much
more closely allied with intellect, if not identical
with it, than is the exaltation of the senses and

the emotions upon which vivid pictorial and
musical effect depends. In short, ever since
the eighteenth century, literature has been becoming less and less intellectual.

Nor, on the other hand, was the eighteenth
century familiar with imagination in its older
Elizabethan manifestation, which consists at its
best, not so much in graphic vizualisation or
seductive melody—though it practises them
too—as in a kind of heightened spiritual perception or penetration which dissolves into its essential unreality the whole world of appearances,
together with the very phantasms and eidola
by which it succeeds in expressing itself. Compare, for instance, what will undoubtedly be
conceded Pope's highest flight, the closing lines
of the *Dunciad* :

> She comes! she comes! the sable throne behold
> Of night primeval, and of Chaos old!
> Before her, fancy's gilded clouds decay,
> And all its varying rainbows die away.
> Thus at her fell approach, and secret might,
> Art after art goes out, and all is night.
> Nor public flame, nor private dares to shine;
> Nor human spark is left, nor glimpse divine!
> Lo! thy dread empire, Chaos! is restored;
> Light dies before thy uncreating word;
> Thy hand, great Anarch! lets the curtain fall,
> And universal darkness buries all:—

compare these lines with the following of
Shakespeare's :

> Out, out, brief candle!
> Life 's but a walking shadow, a poor player
> That struts and frets his hour upon the stage
> And then is heard no more: it is a tale
> Told by an idiot, full of sound and fury,
> Signifying nothing.

Such utterances as this were quite out of the way of Pope and his fellows. They are not quite out of our way; there are reverberations of them through the nineteenth century, feeble by comparison but in the same key. Nothing like them, however, occurs from Dryden to Johnson. The nearest I can think of are things like this:

> Oh had I courage but to meet my fate,
> That short dark passage to a future state,
> That melancholy riddle of a breath!
> That something, or that nothing, after death!

And how remote even this is! The highest flights of the time are, in reality, flights of eloquence rather than of poetry. The close of the *Dunciad* itself is rather eloquent than poetic. And that is the reason, it seems to me, that Dryden has reached points of greater elevation than Pope—because Dryden was naturally eloquent. In some such way as this may be explained the curious similarity of tone as between Dryden and Corneille; for as a general thing eloquence seems to be the noblest modern expression of a strictly classical age or nature.

VI

But though the poetry of the eighteenth century lacked imagination, it possessed one faculty which is sadly to seek at present. It had a very keen sense for ethical ideas. For broad moral generalisation, like that of Greek tragedy, it had doubtless little sympathy and still less capacity. There was nothing cosmical about its point of view. But to everything that bore upon the character and the conduct of the individual in society it was very sensitive. And to modern criticism, curiously enough, it is this strong, if limited moral sense which has proved its most disconcerting feature. There is no word more often in the mouths of the writers of the age than the word nature. Nature, they assert, is their standard; it is nature which they pretend to imitate. "First follow nature," says Pope, repeating the commonplace of his day. And yet to all appearance, if there is anything in which the century seems deficient, it is a feeling for nature as we understand it. Nor, on the other hand, could anything appear less natural than their language and sentiments. Pope's pastorals, we are told, might have been written by a blind man for all the direct observation they show of the subject; while his vocabulary is about three parts convention and artifice. To account for this apparent discrepancy between

profession and practice a great number of explanations have been proposed, some of them
ingenious but all more or less unsatisfactory.
It has been pointed out that by their own con-
fession nature was nothing but a paraphrase
for the imitation of their classics.

> Vos exemplaria Græca
> Nocturna versate manu, versate diurna.

> Learn hence for ancient rules a just esteem,
> To copy nature is to copy them.

Or worse, their pretended deference for nature
has been treated as an empty formula to which
they themselves never thought of attaching any
significance, unless it were as a cover for their
artificiality. More suggestively, however, Leslie
Stephen has observed that the natural, after all,
is nothing more or less than the usual. What
we are used to seems natural, and contrariwise.
And in just the same way that it seems natural
to an Englishman that a soldier should wear a
red coat and unnatural that he should wear any
other; so the poetry of Pope, which seems unnatural to us, seemed quite natural to his contemporaries, while our poetry, which seems
natural to us, would have seemed unnatural to
Pope. And the remark is valuable. On the
score of use and wont it disposes of a great part
of our charges against the artificiality of the
eighteenth century; for I suppose that no one

will maintain that Shakespeare's poetry is any more properly a natural product than is Pope's, or that Zola's *Lourdes*, which is the very *decalque* of actuality, is any better literature than Shakespeare's *Midsummer Night's Dream*, which lies outside of the natural altogether. So it is that Dr. Johnson, who is ridiculed for his own artificiality by Lowell, ridicules Cowley on the same score; while Shakespeare, whom we extol for his naturalness, is denounced for his artificiality by Dryden. In fact, there was never an age that was not artificial to some other and natural to itself. But while this is quite true, Leslie Stephen's suggestion fails to hit the mark. It fails to explain how the poetry of Pope, though it might have seemed natural in this one sense to its *habitués* when once established, should ever have succeeded in recommending itself to any one in the first instance or in justifying its own pretensions as an imitation of nature.

As a matter of fact the difficulty is entirely of our own raising and is due to one of our modern "scientific" confusions. By nature we have come to understand the physical order almost exclusively, the material universe together with the sentient world as far as the latter constitutes a dependency of the former. The natural, therefore, is restricted in our sense to the mechanical and the instinctive or impulsive. Landscape, what was once called "external nature," the

animal and the vegetable, are natural still. It
is natural apparently to act like a beast; quite
unnatural to act like a man. It is in this sense
that Renan declares that nature has no regard
for chastity—or in other words that chastity is
unnatural and hence monstrous. As an inevitable consequence it is held almost universally
nowadays that such of our institutions and be-
liefs, moral, social, political, and the like, as can
not be accounted for by some purely physical
explanation, are necessarily idle, illusory, and
invalid. Morality must be utilitarian, or it is
superstition. And finally it is seriously proposed to apply the methods of "natural" science
to the study of society, of history, even of literature, and of humanity as a whole, in total forget-
fulness apparently that there is another nature
than that of natural science. With such notions
in our heads it is no wonder if we miss the sense
of the eighteenth century. For this conception
of nature, in which we have allowed ourselves to
become wholly absorbed to the exclusion of any
other, the makers of English classicism never
possessed at all. The only kind of nature that
they knew or cared anything about was human
nature. The physical order as such had no
particular significance for them. As a subject
of literature, and particularly of poetry, it was
virtually non-existent. On the one hand they
had no scientific turn, and on the other they

12

had no fondness for those vague impressions,
those unclear and illimitable suggestions and
troubled ideas which we have learned to dote
upon in a cloud or a sunset or a hazy mountain
prospect. What they were concerned for and
what they conceived to be the proper theme of
literature, was the human in its characteristic
and distinctive manifestations. The dubious
affiliations of man with rock, and tree, and stone,
the survivals of a remote and bestial parentage,
"*la bête humaine*" or *végétale*, the eclipse partial
or total of conscience, atavism—all these ambiguous matters that are interesting us so much just
at present, they set aside or overlooked altogether. Human nature in its typical aspects,
as modified by society and culture, with a well-
marked sense for character and conduct, as a
moral intelligence, such was their interest and
their theme. And on this point the evidence of
Dr. Johnson is conclusive.

But the truth is, that the knowledge of external nature, and the sciences which that knowledge requires
or includes, are not the great or the frequent business of
the human mind. Whether we provide for action or
conversation, whether we wish to be useful or pleasing,
the first requisite is the religious and moral knowledge
of right and wrong; the next is an acquaintance with
the history of mankind, and with those examples which
may be said to embody truth, and prove by events the
reasonableness of opinions.   Prudence and justice are
virtues of all times and of all places; we are perpetually

moralists, but we are geometricians only by chance.
Our intercourse with intellectual nature is necessary;
our speculations upon matter are voluntary and at
leisure.

Wise and admirable words! The first requisite is the knowledge of right and wrong. Alas!
that we should have forgotten it in our lives and
have been so eager to substitute in our education
such studies exclusively as furnish a knowledge
of our material surroundings and a technical
dexterity in dealing with them for such as might
serve to form the character and control the
conduct. And this is the reason that the writings
of the eighteenth century would be so salutary for us, if we would only read them. In the
prevalence of the industrial idea we have pretty
well forgotten that there is such a thing as morality, that life is aught but business or amenable
to other than its dingy and dubious standards.
To struggle against the current of an entire
civilisation is impossible; but no less is it wise
and wholesome to escape occasionally from an
atmosphere of this sort into an age in which
every writer was or sought to be a moralist in
concerning himself mainly for correct ideas about
right living. Dryden, Addison, Swift, Pope—
they are all substantially in accord with Dr.
Johnson. Of Shakespeare Dryden says: "He
needed not the spectacle of books to read nature;
he looked inwards and found her there." "The

proper study of mankind is man," declares Pope. In this sense every great literature is moral: it is concerned first and foremost for human nature; it is, as Matthew Arnold says, a criticism of life; and its perusal results in sound ideas about character and conduct.

But the literature of the eighteenth century was moral in an even more obvious and didactic sense than this. It was indeed a criticism of life—not in any such metaphorical sense as that in which Matthew Arnold declares Keats's line,

> Forever wilt thou love and she be fair,

to be a criticism of life, but in a very exact and literal sense. It was critical not only in intention but also in method. The poet of the time believed it his duty to analyse and divide, to comment and moralise, to separate the good from the evil and hold them up to contemplation as such, the one to praise and emulation, the other to ridicule and detestation. Hence his poetry was of a strongly disputatious stamp. It was intended to discuss and argue moral questions and was expected to instruct and edify. Even when its purpose is not so patently pedagogical, it is always more or less conscious of some such conception of its poetic function.

Since I have raised to myself so great an audience, says Addison, speaking, in this instance as in so many others, for his age in speaking for himself, I shall spare no pains to make their instruction agreeable, and their

diversion useful. For which reasons I shall endeavour
to enliven morality with wit, and temper wit with
morality, that my readers may, if possible, both ways
find their account in the speculation of the day. And
to the end that their virtue and discretion may not be
short, transient, intermittent starts of thought, I have
resolved to refresh their memories from day to day, till
I have rescued them out of that desperate state of vice
and folly into which the age is fallen.

Such is their professed aim with hardly an
exception. Even the later novelists lay claim
to it. And if the claim is in some cases a pretence, a mere form of words, as it surely is with
Fielding and Smollett, even then it shows what
a hold the conception had acquired. In fact,
it might not be impossible to deduce all the literary forms of the period from this one principle.
Even the restoration comedy of manners, from
which many of them derive directly or indirectly,
though it seems itself to have taken leave of
morality entirely, has its roots in the same soil—
an interest in the social creature. And if that
comedy perished, or rather transmigrated, it
did so in part because it had ceased to represent
the social being in accordance with the fair sense
of the general public regarding him. It would
take too long to attempt to trace the affiliations
of the various *genres;* but it is easy to observe
the moral essay of Addison and the poetic satire
assuming certain of the social functions of the
comedy of manners as far as that comedy is

ideally a criticism of society and transforming them by the admixture of a didactically moral purpose; while it is still easier to detect in Fielding's novel certain other such functions, at the same time that Richardson picks up the Addisonian essay and by a change of proportions, in enlarging the anecdotal and illustrative portions and reducing the critical and discoursive, produces *Clarissa Harlowe*. But at all events this one point is clear—the culmination of the movement resulted in a serious confusion of poetical and critical methods. And to this cause is referable in the main the relative inferiority of its poetry.

Insist upon the imitation of nature as he might, the poet of the eighteenth century never supposed that the imitation of nature, even understanding by nature human or social nature, was the whole story. Such an idea was of much later origin. It has been reserved for naturalism and the late nineteenth century to assert the identity of life and literature. The classical age knew better. Nothing could be clearer than Dryden's recognition of this fundamental distinction; nothing sharper than his discrimination between the foundation and the aim of literature. As for its materials, poetry is to be tried by the closeness of its imitation—that is, by verisimilitude; as for its purpose, that is quite another matter. "It is true that to imitate well is a

poet's work; but to affect the soul and to excite
the passions; and above all to move admiration,
which is the delight of serious plays, a bare
imitation will not serve." And it is on this
ground exactly, the distinction between life and
literature, that he urges the use of the couplet
in tragedy. "The converse [conversation] therefore, which a poet is to imitate, must be heightened with all the arts and ornaments of poetry;
and must be such, as, strictly considered, could
never be supposed spoken by any without premeditation." Upon this point he insists: a
tragedy is not life; it is a representation of life
from a particular point of view with the aim of
producing a particular effect. Accordingly he
denies—and the denial is an excellent example of
his hard-headed sagacity—he denies explicitly
the statement that "a play will be supposed
to be a composition of several persons speaking
extempore." On the contrary, he boldly declares, "a play is supposed to be the work of the
poet, imitating or representing the conversation
of several persons." Clearly, then, tragedy, is
not intended to diarise our daily existence, but
to "produce," as Goethe says, "the illusion of
a higher reality." What tragedy shall admit,
therefore, is to be decided, not by its exact conformity with nature, but by its suitability to the
particular purpose. For this reason, because
"the plot, the characters, the wit, the passions,

the descriptions are all exalted above the level
of common converse," Dryden advocates the
use in tragedy of the heroic couplet, for, he asks,
if "blank verse is acknowledged to be too low
for a poem . . . how much more for tragedy?"

Such is the position originally taken by Dryden in the great dispute concerning the relative
dramatic merits of blank verse and heroic couplets.   No doubt his mind was somewhat imposed
upon by the example of French tragedy.   But
it is evident at the same time that his mistaken
preference for rhyme is due, not to his misconception of the character of the drama, but to his
misconception of the character of blank verse.
The question with him always reduced itself to
this, that the only possible objection to couplets
was their unnaturalness.   Whereto he replied
that tragedy should raise dialogue above the
tone of natural conversation, as is perfectly
right, and that blank verse was too much like
prose to answer the purpose, as was quite wrong.
What confirms his general position with reference
to tragedy itself is the fact that blank verse
has finally been accepted on the very grounds
whereon he rejected it, because it is felt as the
only measure possessing the requisite loftiness
for tragedy.   And in fact, as his own understanding of English literature increased and his
appreciation of its genius improved, he gave
up the couplet himself and took to blank verse

more or less successfully. In the beginning,
however, it is only fair to remember, he was in
reality attempting to produce a kind of illusion
quite different from that of Shakespeare and
what has turned out to be our traditional poetic
drama, and this he succeeded in a sense in doing
for a while in the heroic play.

To this extent, then, it seems clear that Dryden and his successors understood what literature is or ought to be. Indeed, one of the most
striking characteristics of their period as compared with ours is their strong literary sense.
We may have more feeling for "life" and "nature" nowadays, especially for their picturesque
and panoramic aspects. But as compared with
theirs our sense of literature is weak and insecure.
At least they read, and they knew the difference
between literature and journalism, that close
transcription of actuality which forms almost
exclusively the present conception of literature.
If they imitated anything, it was rather the
spectacle of life as it is mirrored in the consciousness of the reflective moral being; and it was the
illusion of a moral order so acquired which they
tried to reproduce. This illusion—the illusion,
in Goethe's words, of a higher reality—is not to
be produced by copying our sensations, but by
selecting and grouping certain of them into a
complete and satisfactory whole in accordance
with some idea that the poet has made for him-

self of their significance and meaning. To be sure, these elements should resemble in some measurable way the materials of experience, though it is a matter of indifference whether they are fact or not. But if he merely reproduce his observations, he will in like manner reproduce only the sensations proper to them, the strained, bewildered sense of actuality; he will produce no illusion at all. His work is valueless; it is true neither in a higher nor a lower sense; it is neither fact nor illusion. A matter is worth saying for either of two reasons: either because it is so, or because it is significant. But as the data of a poem are fictitious, the poem itself can not be of value for the former reason. It must, then, depend for its value upon its significance. But it is evident that the only significance which literature can possess must be due to the general conception of life which it embodies—that is, to an idea. Even its verisimilitude, its measurable resemblance to reality, depends rather upon conformity with the idea than upon conformity with fact: "it is a false tendency," says Goethe, "to push the resemblance so far that nothing but a vulgar reality remains." The sense of reality proper to poetry is due mainly to the consistency of the detail with the principle of the poem—that is, it is in part a reflection of the illusion itself and of the general significance of the poem as a whole,

for what is intelligible is likely to be mistaken
for real. And at the same time and what
amounts to much the same thing in the end, it
results in part from the self-consistency of the
detail as it builds up an experience which is
again felt as real in as far as it is complete and
significant in itself.

Finally, therefore, literature is always a matter of ideas; and since it deals with human life
and conduct, a matter consequently of moral
ideas. So far it seems perfectly proper with
Matthew Arnold to consider poetry a criticism
of life. In another aspect, however, the attitude is less satisfactory and is likely to introduce
a confusion, the direct contrary of that involved
in naturalism or *l'art pour l'art*, but no less serious on that account. For the methods as well
as the ultimate aims of poetry and criticism are
thoroughly incompatible. The final object of
criticism consists in disengaging the idea from
the various accidents and circumstances with
which it is invested in consciousness and in holding it up to steady contemplation by itself;
while the object of poetry, on the contrary,
consists in the incorporation of the idea in such
a set of accidents and circumstances as will
produce a sense of higher or significant reality.
In other words, criticism seeks to dispel the illusion which it is the very purpose of poetry to
produce. What the latter attempts to embody,

the former tries to isolate. And while there is no illusion without an idea to give it significance, there is equally no illusion without some semblance to reality to serve as a foundation. In short, we are poets and romancers by nature, but critics only by profession. While we inform our life with illusion instinctively, our criticism, in a deliberate attempt to see the thing "as in itself it really is," renounces at once illusion and poetry.

Such, however, is the natural consequence of romantic excess. The more irresponsible and sensational a poetry allows itself to become, just so much the more violent is the inevitable classical reaction. Literature is always in extremes. And after a period of dissipation and extravagance, it is only to be expected that Pope and his contemporaries, like Matthew Arnold in our own day, should over-emphasise the critical function of poetry. In recognising the importance of moral ideas they were doing good service to literature. Their mistake lay in attempting to apply to the treatment of these ideas the methods of criticism rather than those of poetry. In those kinds of literature which are most nearly akin to criticism they are accordingly at their best—in the essay and prose generally, which is essentially critical in character, and in the satire and whatever poetry is properly didactic or philosophical. But they seldom produce an illusion, because they fail to give their ideas the form and semblance of reality. Such as they were, however, they corrected our literature of the mediævalism which still clung to it, and they established a sound prose tradition for the language in much the same way that Shakespeare may be said to have established our national poetic tradition.

MAUPASSANT IN ENGLISH

IT is only ten years since Maupassant was buried—on Saturday, July 8, 1893, as Goncourt records in the Journal, "in the Church of Chaillot, where I saw Louise L. married." And already our attention, like his friend's, has begun to turn elsewhere. Nor is there, indeed, very much in Maupassant to attach us permanently. His vision of life is contemptible. And as for his ideas—of any considerable body of literary work that has ever made its way in the world, his, with the possible exception of Gautier's, contains the smallest modicum of intellect. In these respects his work is so foreign to the genius and the ideals of our own literature that it has hitherto received but partial and unsatisfactory treatment at the hands of English translators. It is only at this rather late day, when his fame has already declined a little, that we are finally promised a thoroughly definitive version in fifteen volumes, handsomely illustrated, and preceded by an introduction by M. Bourget.[1]   By the excellence

[1] *The Complete Works of Guy de Maupassant* Rendered into English by a Corps of Distinguished Translators, with a Critical Preface by Paul Bourget,

of its details, both literary and mechanical, as
well as by its completeness, this edition bids
fair to attract a good deal of attention to its
author. And for this reason it seems desirable
to undertake some more exact characterisation
of his work as a whole and to estimate its value
from the point of view of the literature into
which it is about to be naturalised.

Like Flaubert, then, whom he styles "Master,"
and whom he strikingly resembles in several
respects, Maupassant seems to have been
dominated exclusively by an obsession of the
bête, a mixture of vulgarity, ignorance, and
fatuity almost impossible of translation, which
had for him a snaky horror and fascination. He
is like his master also in the practice of a rigid
"imperturbability"—heartlessness, we should
call it; only, while Flaubert was occasionally
carried away by a great enthusiasm, there is
never the faintest glimmer of moral sense in all
Maupassant's uncleanly pages. And yet his
cynicism is not entirely without relief. The
constant preoccupation with the mean, the
trivial, and the commonplace tends, particularly
in the case of a sensitive nature, to induce an undue respect for the petty as well as an undue
contempt for it. And in the midst of his con-
temptuous indifference to the miseries of exist-

of the French Academy. Fifteen Volumes. Illustrated. New York: M. Walter Dunne.

ence, it is not uncommon to come across some lean streak of feeling—a humour or a pathos so rudimentary and animal that it makes his cynicism appear enlightened in comparison. He "fixes a hard eye," says Mr. Henry James, "on some small spot of human life, usually some ugly, dreary, shabby, sordid one, takes up the particle, and squeezes it either till it grimaces or till it bleeds." But rather the wound, if it must be, than the smirk—the frank brutality of *L'Héritage* than the ambiguous sentimentality of *Boule de Suife*. His favourite subject is the peasant—perhaps because it gratified the taste for *saleté*, for the malodorous, which, like most of his contemporaries, he shared with Baudelaire—the peasant and the *petit bourgeois*, the lower middle class, whose sensuality is aggravated by a life of airless and unnatural confinement. At the bottom of his cup there is always this one motive, which relieves him from making any very elaborate psychology about his figures, twitched as they all are by a single unmentionable appetite. No doubt in this way, by eliminating the moral element entirely and reducing life to the dimensions of a primary instinct, he was able to give an amazing concision and rapidity, a marvellous saliency and relief to what remained. But, aside from the purely secondary consideration that it makes discussion of his work almost impossible in English except

in a very general fashion, his simplicity is
dearly bought. It distorts his scheme of creation to the figure of a grotesque; and, what
seems worse, though it amounts to the same
thing in the end, it confines his literary activity
to the exercise of a particularly narrow and
exclusive art.

For art, as it touches life, is to a great extent
a matter of proportion. It is hardly necessary
for the writer to eschew the evil for the sake of
delineating only the good; the result would still
be distortion of a kind to which we English are
too prone already, and of which Dickens's
gingerly treatment of little Emily is still a
pretty fair example. But as a whole his vision
of the world ought to bear some recognisable
relation to the human spectacle, which he pretends to represent, particularly if he has produced more than a hundred tales and half a
dozen novels; for, though things may be very
much worse in France than they are in America,
it is difficult to believe them quite so bad as
Maupassant makes out. And yet the fundamental weakness of his work is not its baseness
after all—that we might be able to tolerate
if it meant anything—but its irrelevance.
Une Vie for instance, is not a very offensive
book in comparison with *Bel Ami;* it is only,
like most of its author's, a perfectly meaningless one. The former is merely the story of a

13

woman, a pitiable, pathetic creature, who lives
but to be duped in every relation of life, as a
wife, a mother, and a daughter, and who at last,
orphaned, widowed, childless, and disabused,
settles down, for the remainder of her days, in
a cottage by the wayside, to the contemplation of the dull, undeviating turnpike before
her door.   The latter, on the contrary, relates
the career of a Parisian journalist, who makes
his way in the world by his good looks and the
frailty of women, discarding his instruments one
after the other as they have served his turn,
until he finally establishes himself by marrying
the daughter of one of his former benefactresses
—an atrocious dénouement on which Maupassant
has spared no pains.   And yet, different as they
are in motive, the two novels are as insignificant the one as the other.   To take only their
conclusions—the long white road which leads
nowhere, as far as the poor broken woman in
Une Vie is concerned, and on which the folk go
back and forth, growing and dwindling, as aim-
lessly to her as the flies on the ceiling—the
thousand trivial little incidents that scatter
and distract her days, to say nothing of her
listless memories of the past, are all as senseless
as the elaborate bridal circumstance which
serves for culmination to *Bel Ami*—the horses
and carriages, the crowd of spectators and
invited guests, the procession and ceremonial—

and which would not be misplaced in the social
columns of a daily paper. They are both excellent pieces of prose in themselves, though the
former is very much the better; but they both
lack that higher relevancy which comes only
from a sense of the significance of the subject.
For what are all these details to us—what does
it matter how a purely factitious character, a
man or a woman in a book, may spend the time
in low intrigue or witless bemusement, unless
there be involved in these incidents some
principle or philosophy of life so clear, so convincing, that its application is unavoidable? It
is not the exactitude of the facts that we care for,
it is the pertinency of the example. And, in
spite of his reputation as a painter of reality,
it is just this vital connection between art and
life which Maupassant fails to catch and hold,
and, missing this, misses the mark completely.
For further explanations, however, we must turn
to our author himself.

The only demand, he says in the introduction
to *Pierre et Jean*, which the critic has a right
to make of the artist, is that he produce "something fine in the form that suits him best according to his temperament." "What child's
play," he goes on after an interval, "to believe in
reality when we each carry our own reality in our
thoughts and organs! Our eyes, our ears, our
sense of smell and taste, differing from one

another's, create as many truths as there are
men on earth." And further: "Each of us,"
therefore, "creates for himself an illusion of
the world, which is poetic or sentimental or
joyous or melancholy or unclean or lugubrious,
according to his temperament, and the writer
has no other mission than to reproduce faithfully this illusion with all the contrivances of
art which he has learned and can dispose of."
Now what is so very mischievous here is not exactly this assertion of temperament, but rather
the divorce between art and every serious concern of spirit, as though art were a sort of
adscititious embellishment, and had nothing
whatever to do with the creation and correction
of the illusion, which literature is merely to
embody. The character of the illusion, sentimental, unclean, or lugubrious, is apparently a
matter of perfect indifference; what makes the
artist is, not the ability to inform it with meaning, but solely the ability to reproduce it; while
as for the critic, Maupassant declares that he
must be "without preconceived opinions";
he must "judge the product only in accordance
with the nature of the effort"; he must take
no cognisance of "tendencies," sentiments, or
ideas; he must have no notion what a piece of
work ought to be like; in short he must remain
dead to the whole conception. "A critic who
would really merit the name ought . . . [only] to

take account of the artistic value of the object
of art submitted to him." Very pretty! Only,
after the ideas, opinions, tendencies, and conceptions of an object of art are set aside, what
in the world remains to constitute the "art" and
to be taken account of—unless it is the mere
facture, the mechanics and technique of the
thing, which is solely a matter of materials and
the affair, in any just sense of language, not of
artist, but of artisan? In short, this introduction is clearly the performance of a man without
genuine literary vocation in the strict sense—
one, that is, who has no meanings to express, no
views of life to commemorate, who considers
writing merely as a craft, and literature as
nothing more than an exercise in the technical
elements of style.

This, then, is Maupassant's conception of
literature as expressed in his own words, and
it needs no very profound knowledge of his
work to recognise that this was also his practice.
One becomes only the more convinced, the more
one studies him, that style was his sole concern,
and that his illusion was only a reflection of life,
as adventitious and arbitrary as the original
itself. Even his cynicism is the inadvertent
cynicism of accident, and depends largely on
the incongruity of circumstances. If there
seems at first sight to be a significance of choice
in his themes, as though he believed the world

in truth to be as sordid as he represents, and picked his subjects accordingly, this apparent significance resolves on consideration into an instinctive preference for the kind of thing that he could do best. Nor is it possible, on the other hand, to overlook from page to page traces of a deliberate effort to obliterate what vestiges of intelligent design have slipped into his creation, and to give his mimic world an air of wanton and irresponsible fortuity. One novel there is in particular, if it be permissible to speak of it, where this sense of the insignificance, the unreality of art, breaks out with unmistakable distinctness. In *Fort comme la Mort*, a painter, who has been engaged for a number of years in a *liaison* with a woman of the world, falls desperately in love with her daughter on the eve of the latter's marriage. Possessed by the charm of her youth and the reflection of her mother's earlier graces, he becomes ever more unable to reconcile himself to the approaching wedding, when, happily for his reason, he is run over in the street and killed, in the very nick of time. Now it may be Philistine, but it is surely natural, to inquire the meaning of this ambiguous and unpleasant complication, and the accident that is obliging enough to put an end to it. There seems, as usual, to be no design blown in the bottle, which exists to all appearance for the sake of a few lines sharply etched on the surface of the glass.

"The highest problem of every art," says Goethe, "consists in representing things in such a way as to produce the illusion of a higher reality. It is a false tendency, however, when representation is pushed so far that nothing but a common reality remains." In this respect, therefore, Maupassant succeeds in producing no illusion, no effect of a genuine or "higher reality" at all. Perhaps, in spite of his own words, he never actually aimed to do so. But at all events, whatever he intended, it was inevitable that, with his disregard for everything save the distracting coruscations of style, he should succeed only in reproducing something of the crude emotion, the bewilderment, and perplexity of life as it comes up before the senses, dazzling and disorderly. Take for example this bit of descriptive writing:

But soon the horse's jerky trot set the car to jolting so badly that the chairs began to dance, and the passengers to toss from side to side, puppet-like, with scared grimaces and frightened cries, suddenly interrupted by some bump more violent than usual. They clutched the sides of the vehicle, with their bonnets flapped over upon their backs or noses or shoulders, while the white horse jogged on, stretching out his head and stiffening the little tail, hairless as a rat's, with which he occasionally whisked his buttocks. Joseph Rivet, with one foot thrust out on the shaft and the other leg folded

under him, held the reins, his elbows cocked high, and
kept uttering a little throaty cluck, which made the
nag prick up his ears and quicken his pace.   On either
side of the road spread the green country.   In spots
the flowering *colza* made an undulating yellow carpet,
whence rose a wholesome smell, penetrating and pleasant, borne afar by the breeze.   The corn-flowers raised
their little heads amid the tall rye—but though the
women would have gathered some, M. Rivet refused
to stop.   Here and there a whole field was so covered
with poppies that it looked as though it were sprinkled
with blood.   And in the midst of this expanse, gathering colour from the flowers of the field, moved the cart,
like a more brilliant nosegay, to the jogging of the white
horse.   It vanished behind the trees of a farm, to reap-
pear where the foliage thinned anew and to pass again
by green and yellow crops variegated with hues of blue
and red—dwindling gradually away in the sunshine
with its gaudy load of women.

This is what Mr. James calls an "admirable
vignette"; and in this one particular, in the
expression, as Goethe says, of "a common
reality," it cannot be denied that Maupassant
does touch a kind of greatness—or at least a
kind of distinction. His senses were extraor-
dinarily keen; and his writing is spangled with
numerous little images of almost crystalline
hardness and brilliancy, like particles of quartz
and mica in a gravel path. Anything that
offered an edge or a surface, the ordures of Paris
or the paunch of a *bourgeois*, a stigma or a
deformity, he was certain of catching with a
vividness hardly less than marvellous. For

this reason his figures, though they stand for
little or nothing, have a solidity, a plasticity,
which is not Greek, though there is nothing
else to compare it with. In fact, so far does he
carry this method of portraiture that it is a fair
question whether he was not capable of gratui-
tous distortion, as he was of partial selection,
for the sake of enhancing the poignancy of his
expression. A writer's real theory usually consists in the discovery of the kind of thing that
he can do best; and it was, as a matter of practice, in the superficial adjustment between expression and the sharp somatic thrill of things,
the smart and tingle of sensation, that he set
his ambition, without other care than just this
rather unintelligent one, for the significance of
his subject. To this effect he quotes Flaubert
with ingenuous approval:

" When you pass," he [Flaubert] used to say, "a grocer
sitting at the door of his shop, a janitor smoking his
pipe, a stand of hackney coaches, show me that grocer
and that janitor, their attitudes, their whole physical
appearance, embracing, likewise, as indicated by the
skilfulness of the picture, their whole moral nature, so
that I cannot confound them with any other grocer or
any other janitor. Make me see, in one word, that a
certain cab horse does not resemble the fifty others that
follow or precede it."

This was his ideal—the thing he actually
tried to do; and *La Maison Tellier*, from which
I recently quoted, is probably his most success-

ful realisation of it. "I perceived," he observes toward the close of his essay on the novel—and the contrast with Zola's notion of "big machines" is remarkable—"that the best writers have very seldom left more than one volume; and that before all things it is necessary to have the opportunity of finding, amid the multiplicity of matters presented to our choice, that which will absorb all our faculties, all our work, and all our artistic powers." *La Maison Tellier* fortunately fills no volume, but it is the result of some such favourable coincidence as this. The subject, which is as usual quite unspeakable, seems to have been singularly well adapted to his temperament and his technique, and the story is, therefore, thoroughly representative of his peculiar powers—a work hard, senseless, and irrelevant, but, according to his own definition, "short, unique, and as perfect as it can possibly be made." As a novelist, however, he was never quite so successful. He could evoke a moment with admirable assurance, assembling detail, incident, and circumstance into a lively, though not always a very congruous, whole. But he never discovered the important truth that at least in one respect the novel, like all forms of epical relation, resembles history. Its framework is indeed composed of a number of critical moments, "Crusoe recoiling from the footprint, Achilles shouting over against the

Trojans, Ulysses bending the great bow." But the connections between these culminating points or stations, which are few and evident in the story, require in the case of the novel as in that of history an unravelling of motives, a following of subterraneous clues, a logical and philosophical sort of research, in short a recognition of the ideal, which was not very much to Maupassant's taste. And yet in spite of this relative inferiority it is grateful, in closing, to dwell for a moment on *Pierre et Jean*, which is the most satisfactory of all his work, even if it is not the most perfect, just because it is an exception and does result in some intelligible sense of human character and conduct.

CORNEILLE: THE NEO-CLASSIC TRAGEDY AND THE GREEK

I

IT is not solely the fault of our critics that we have no such criticism as the French; it is also the fault of our literature. To write a history of English literature like M. Lanson's history of French literature is, even on that small scale, impossible from the nature of the subject. To be sure, there is no such general interest in the former as in the latter. The historian or the critic who undertakes French letters finds an opinion already formed, a canon already established. His meal is at least partly ground for him; he has only to make his dough. But this is not all the difference. English literature, unlike the French, does not constitute a coherent body of thought, a consistent "criticism of life," with a fairly continuous growth or evolution; and a similar treatment of it, as a branch of intellectual development, is therefore out of the question. In fact, our literature is not so largely an affair of definition; not only is it poorer in ideas, it is also patterned less closely in accordance with theory. In all English there

is no example of the *genre tranché*, such as Sainte-
Beuve loved; hardly of a conscious school or
formula, or even of a preconceived purpose.
It is individual, capricious, empiric, indiscriminate. The writer himself seems hardly conscious
of his own inclination, but follows instinctively the line of least resistance. Not only is
the Shakespearean comedy utterly promiscuous,
compounded of many simples, a thing without
prescription; it is also more or less a thing apart,
without a history, itself a "sport" like the genius
which produced it. To the student of English,
for whom such work has become standard, it
is something of a surprise to read Corneille with
Voltaire's commentary at hand and observe
the nicety with which the critic pretends to discriminate among his author's ingredients, not
merely as they are good or bad, but as they are
agreeable or otherwise with the literary type before him. It is a revelation of the comparative
precision and purity of the ideas in accordance
with which French literature was, and in spite
of the confusions of the *romanticists* still is, to
some extent, written and judged.

But at the same time, definite as are the lines
on which French literature moves, the symmetry
of the French classic at all events, and of the
classic French drama in particular, is likely to
appear rather rigid and formal to the student
of English. And yet there is one side by which

Corneille and even Racine may appeal to him. With an instinct of definiteness and regularity which is peculiarly French, their work combines singularly enough something of that promiscuity, of that anomalousness, which he is used to in English, though with a difference. For it is not the mere adaptation of a foreign or an ancient model which is characteristic of that particular literature. Indeed, if it were nothing else than an imitation of the pure classic, like Milton's *Samson Agonistes*, the neo-classic drama would be of comparatively little interest. As a matter of fact, however, it was an attempt to interpret one life in terms evolved by another. Naturally the new wine tended to dilate, even to disrupt, the old bottles, while conforming to their general outline. But since a literary form is not merely a vehicle of thought but an outgrowth of it; the attempt, such as it was in other respects, necessarily involved, in their application to new uses, a criticism of the terms themselves and of the ancient ideas implicit in them. And it is this fusion, or rather this collision of two cultures in the one set of expressions, with all its complicated discrepancies and contradictions, which constitutes the peculiarity of the neo-classic tragedy. In fact, so peculiar is it that the reader who approaches it from the side of an integral tradition, however heterogeneous the latter may be, hardy knows what to make of it at first, and will never, the chances are, acquire a genuine taste for it.

While in Racine's case it is the product as a whole which the foreigner finds disconcerting, yet in Corneille's the feeling of individual incongruities is perhaps the more noticeable. To the English reader in particular, if I am successful in recalling an original impression, Corneille presents at first sight a sufficiently curious spectacle. As a great spontaneous genius—for such, however outlandish to us in manner, he certainly was—capable both of the happiest turns and the flattest lapses, he finds his nearest English counterpart in Shakespeare, though in the ethic appreciation of character and in the phantasmagoric sense of life he was so far inferior. For this reason it is unsafe to judge Corneille before one has taken his range. He is not a poet to be measured by any one piece, even by that perfectly unique masterpiece of irony and statescraft, *Nicomède;* for he never succeeded in attaining a level and keeping it. There are always times when his hand is out. He has his ups and downs at every period, in nearly every play. His development is not rectilinear and continuous, but radial and spasmodic. And it is necessary, in order to know him, not merely to establish the *loci* of his career chronologically, but also to ascertain his high-water marks and plot his curve from one to another—

the intrigue of *le Menteur*, the rhetoric of *Pompée*, the romance of *le Cid*, and so on. In some such manner alone one comes to understand the elevation to which his spirit rose from time to time. And though it ebbs as often as it touches such an extreme, yet, together with a sense of the instability of his genius, one gains also a sense of its variety and compass, for it recedes merely to flow again in some new direction.

As a bold and vigorous temperament, on the other hand, a Norman, with a taste for the romantic and sensational, for intrigue and adventure, but constrained and embarrassed by the timidity of a conventional and imitative society and age, he approaches most nearly to Dryden, though he lacked the latter's easy adaptability and his thoroughly English common-sense and humour. But for all that there are about the author of *Tyrannick Love* a stiffness, not so much of temper as of craft, an awkwardness and also an imperturbable solemnity in the pursuit of the tragic which are very like the author of *Polyeucte*. Indeed, Dryden is probably, of all English dramatists, the one who resembles Corneille most, whether because he deliberately formed himself upon his illustrious contemporary or was naturally of a kindred spirit. At times when Dryden is at his best, his note is almost identical with certain of Corneille's.

Que tout meure avec moi, madame: que m'importe
Qui foule après ma mort la terre qui me porte?
Sentiront-ils percer par un éclat nouveau,
Ces illustres aïeux la nuit de leur tombeau?
Respireront-ils l'air où les feront revivre
Ces neveux qui peut-être auront peine à les suivre,
Peut-être ne feront que les déshonorer,
Et n'en auront le sang que pour dégénérer?
Quand nous avons perdu le jour qui nous éclaire,
Cette sorte de vie est bien imaginaire,
Et le moindre moment d'un bonheur souhaité
Vaut mieux qu'une si froide et vaine éternité.

Surena, i., 3.

How vain is virtue, which directs our ways
Through certain danger to uncertain praise!
Barren and airy name! thee Fortune flies,
With her lean train, the pious and the wise.
Heaven takes thee at thy word, without regard,
And lets thee poorly be thy own reward.
The world is made for the bold impious man,
Who stops at nothing, seizes all he can.
Justice to merit does weak aid afford;
She trusts her balance and neglects her sword.
Virtue is nice to take what 's not her own;
And while she long consults the prize is gone.

Aureng-Zebe, ii., 1.

La vie est peu de chose; et tôt ou tard qu'importe
Qu'un traître me l'arrache, ou que l'âge l'importe?
Nous mourons à toute heure; et dans le plus doux sort
Chaque instant de la vie est un pas vers la mort.

Tite et Berenice, v., 1.

Decidedly Corneille is the greater playwright.
But it is impossible in his case as in Dryden's
to overlook this significant sense of constraint,

because it is a critical symptom of the *genre* as
it was in that age.   There are writers more artificial than Dryden and Corneille; but there are
few, if any, who produce, with so strong an
impression of power, the same peculiar effect
of *gêne*.   Racine is more artificial and conventional; but Racine has learned to move smoothly
and elegantly within the bounds prescribed him.
He is, to all appearance, happily unconscious of
interference or obstruction.   But in Corneille's
case it is not so much that he is hindered in the
satisfaction of his desires as that he is not quite
sure what he wants himself—or ought to want.
For this state of mind the *Examens* are conclusive.   It is sufficient to quote from that of
Rodogune:

On m'a souvent fait une question à la Cour, quel
étoit celuy de mes poëmes que j'estimois le plus, et
j'ay trouvé tous ceux qui me l'ont faite si prévenus en
faveur de *Cinna* ou du *Cid* que je n'ay jamais osé dé-
clarer toute la tendresse que j'ay toûjours euë pour
celuy-cy, à qui j'aurois volontiers donné ma suffrage,
si je n'avois craint de manquer en quelque sorte au
respect que je devois à ceux que je voyois pancher d'un
autre costé.   Cette préférence est peut-estre en moy
un effet de ces inclinations aveugles qu'ont beaucoup
de péres pour quelques-uns de leurs enfans plus que
pour les autres; peut-estre y entre-t-il un peu d'amour
propre, en ce que cette tragédie me semble estre un peu
plus à moy que celles qui l'ont précédée, à cause des
incidens surprenans qui sont purement de mon invention, et n'avoient jamais été veus au theâtre; et peut-

estre enfin y a-t-il un peu de vray mérite, qui fait que
cette inclination n'est pas tout-à-fait injuste.

It is instructive to compare this tentative
judgment with Lessing's, who was an inveterate
classicist after his kind and knew precisely
what he was after.

Denn wozu alle diese Erdichtungen? Machen sie
in der Geschichte, die er damit überladet, das geringste
wahrscheinlicher? Sie sind nicht einmal für sich selbst
wahrscheinlich. Corneille prahlte damit als mit sehr
wunderbaren Anstrengungen der Erdichtungskraft;
und er hätte doch wohl wissen sollen, dass nicht das
blosse Erdichten, sondern das zweckmässige Erdichten
einen schöpfrischen Geist beweise.

But it is only fair to remark, too, that his
criticism, excellent as it is in method, as well
as the usual present-day estimate, rests upon
a misconception in assuming Cléopatre as the
personage of the piece by whom it necessarily
stands or falls. For the mistake there is the
more excuse because Corneille himself speaks
to the same effect. And yet it seems obvious
enough that the interest does not centre in Cléopatre at all, but in Antiochus. Antiochus, not
Cléopatre, is the genuinely Corneillean character.
And the recognition of this fact requires some
readjustment of criticism.

By the time Corneille had made *Nicomède*
he had, to be sure, developed a kind of formula;
his succeeding plays do follow essentially the

same receipt.　But it is in reality nothing more than a *procédé*, not a theorem, and it does not always work.　All his life he remained virtually divided between impulse and authority, unable to choose definitely, but anxious to effect a reconciliation, between the old and the new, the medieval and the antique—to *accorder les règles anciennes avec les agrémens modernes*, in his own words—in short, between those two conceptions of literature and life which were brought into such violent confrontation by the renaissance and which have since come to be distinguished, rather vaguely though conveniently, as romantic and classic.　Hence the curiously experimental character peculiar to his drama, which is in fact a compromise among the rival claimants to his regard and is consequently full of contradictions and inconsistencies.

II

To define broadly the difference between these two views of literature, it may be said, in very general terms, that the modern or romantic manner has made itself remarkable mainly for its research of actuality.　The thrill and tingle of sensation, the smart of experience, the distraction of accident and circumstance, the harsh and stinging contact of things material—these are the effects it chiefly admires and imitates.

The sole literary development of any importance
since the Greeks has consisted almost wholly in
devices for the more accurate registration of
fact, whether of character or incident, until the
kaleidoscopic spectacle of nature and the parti-
colored phantasmagoria of human life have come
to constitute for modern literature and art the
only serious concern.   To the Greek tragedian,
on the contrary, art was the sole reality, not life;
life itself was merely phantasmal, a vain and
misleading appearance.

Ὁρῶ γὰρ ἡμᾶς οὐδὲν ὄντας ἄλλο πλὴν
εἴδωλ', ὅσοιπερ ζῶμεν, ἢ κούφην ὅκιάν.

Ajax, 125–26.

That it was infinitely poignant, infinitely suggestive, he saw; but he saw also that it was
infinitely prolix, irrelevant, and disconcerting,
and that its poignancy, no less than its suggestiveness, was the result, not of its significance,
but of its indefiniteness.   On the whole such a
vision, by its very confusion and uncertainty,
afflicted him, like a nightmare, with the nameless moral horror which still lurks upon the
confines of the *Prometheus Bound*—the horror
of a man who has just made good his escape
from a world of chaos and unreason.   To his
mind it was in no way desirable that a poem
should be *suggestive*, that it should produce a
vague and tantalising sense of illimitable possibility, but rather that is should be *expressive*—

that it should contain, not so much an exact
reproduction of experience and of the emotions
proper to it, as some principle for its intelligible ordering and interpretation.   In short, the
main affair was the general idea after which the
play was cast.   And it is for this reason that
Greek tragedy always produces a profound
conviction of design.   It is not a free observation or impression of life, as we say nowadays,
giving rise to any number of inferences and
suggestions.   It is an arrangement, an adaptation, set, not to catch an exact image of reality,
but to mirror the author's thought.   It does
not disturb or trouble or distract by the flicker
of its surface reflection or the opacity of its
intention, like *King Lear;* it settles and confirms
and tranquilises, like the *Œdipus*.   And finally
it displaces every other possible interpretation,
informing the consciousness with its own image
and idea to the exclusion of all others.   It is
whole and single and complete, a closed system
which neither admits nor raises conjecture—
at once a cosmos and a revelation.

Even if the Greek had had the pretension to
make his drama a *pastiche* of life, as we do ours,
it is doubtful whether he could ever have succeeded in doing so on account of its peculiar
construction.   The chorus alone would have
been enough to destroy the acute sense of actuality.   To say nothing at present of the temporal

and spatial restrictions which it imposed upon
the action and which were enough in themselves
to divide it from existence and give it an air of
intelligent fabrication—even then, if a bit of
real life could have been exposed there in the
Greek orchestra, it would not have looked real
with the chorus between it and the spectators.
The chorus itself might be conceived as looking
at life directly; but in no case could the audience,
viewing it through the chorus, be conceived as
getting it otherwise than as refracted by the
medium through which it passed, like the report
of a bystander. And such, in all probability,
as De Quincey ingeniously suggests,[1] was in
effect its artistic force. It framed off the representation, setting it apart, if not altogether insu-
lating it, from actual existence, re-enforcing
its idealistic character and at the same time
rationalising what we are prone to consider its
artificiality. For, whether the chorus were tech-
nically spectator or actor, it is clear enough in
any case that Greek tragedy is, by its very
interposition, separated from experience by at
least one more remove than modern tragedy;

---

[1] De Quincey, *The Theory of Greek Tragedy*. *Cf.*
Brunetière, *L'Evolution d'un genre, Études critiques
sur l'histoire de la littérature française*, vii. "Nous
n'avons plus sous les yeaux les événements eux-mêmes,
mais le reflet des événements dans l'imagination du
poète."

and represents, therefore, an additional mental distillation or rectification of fact.

Of course it would be absurd to say that modern literature engages in its productions no ultimate significance at all. If it did not— if it merely imposed upon the phenomena of experience the more or less arbitrary form of some *genre*, as naturalism tries to do—it would, like naturalism, be hardly felt as literature at all. In a comparison of Shakespeare's four tragedies, *Hamlet, Othello, King Lear,* and *Macbeth,* it is curious to observe that the last is dramatically superior to the others, and is at the same time the clearest, the most intelligible in design, and reveals most distinctly the presence of a controlling purpose, the imprint of a definite idea. There is little or no more difficulty about the meaning of *Macbeth* as a whole than about that of the *Ajax*—a circumstance, perhaps, which gives it its deceptive air of similarity to the Greek. On the contrary, *King Lear,* which is the least subservient to such control—for how can any vital congruity be established between the last act and the acts preceding?—is dramatically the least effective and produces what effect it does produce, like life itself, scatteringly and piecemeal, with a final sense of mystification, bewilderment, and agitation. For it must be constantly remembered, in judging of these matters, that a piece which requires for its sig-

nificance the perception of some wider principle
of order than the piece itself declares, is precisely
a fragment of life, not a work of art. And it is
vicious criticism, for instance, to say of *King
Lear* that it is not in itself inconsistent with the
Christian conception of a beneficent overruling
Providence or to refer to its unreason as a case
carried up to some higher court for revision.[1] A
play is significant in itself or not at all. To
Sophocles any mere concatenation of circumstances, such as composes *King Lear*, no matter
how close the mechanical articulation or the
causal connection, would not constitute a drama
unless it yielded a consistent idea.

It is not, then, that romantic literature is
entirely lacking in that purposefulness which
discerns a leading idea amid the ferment of
existence and organises its material accordingly;
it is rather that in modern literature such ideas
have come to play a part subordinate to the
registration of discrete impressions. And yet
this is not the whole story either. Not only
has the influence of ideas decreased, their character has also changed. A literature will
always reflect the sense of its makers. If they
are concerned mainly with their kind, and with
the world which they inhabit only as the theatre

---

[1] Compare A. C. Bradley, *Shakespearean Tragedy*,
lect. viii. This, moreover, is a fallacy which tends
to vitiate Freytag's treatment of the tragic.

of human action, then will their interpretation, as well as their vision of life, be in the main a moral one. But, on the other hand, if they are interested in the universe chiefly for its own sake, as a curious spectacle in which man figures like any other object only that he is locomotory, then will every fact have a value in and for itself irrespective of any ultimate significance; while those who consider curiously will find, no doubt, the meaning of the whole to consist in some idea or expression or formula about the relation of the various parts which appear in themselves so very interesting and important. And their exposition of life, like their conception of it, will be mainly materialistic or, in modern language, scientific. Now some such change as this it is which has, to all appearance, taken place. Whereas the Greek had little or no mechanical sense of fact, the modern has been more and more inclining, in accordance with the latter view, to consider nature itself as of superlative importance, and consciousness as but a small and even subordinate part of it. Hence that growing curiosity about things as things and that supreme confidence in the illusion of physical law and order which are reflected by his literature, on the one hand in the promiscuous reproduction of every sort of sensation and impression, and on the other hand in the suggestion of some outlying mechanical nexus as an all-sufficient principle of literary order. In this sense, however, the world made no appeal to the Greek dramatist. As a mechanical contrivance it left him cold—if such, indeed, it really be. At all events, it had not for him this particularly dreary illusion which has come to form its main significance for us. For this very reason he was able, with far less interest than we take in nature, to see and describe objects much more clearly than we are able to do. He perceived them more nearly as they are—at least in their relation to human life, with which he was himself preoccupied. For his illusion was essentially a moral one. Never would he have fallen into such fatal confusion as did Renan in alleging the unchastity of nature as a criterion of conduct. He was more likely, in the inverse sense, to prescribe to nature from his own conscience. Indeed his religion, which Symonds calls at once a religion and a poetry, was an attempt to animate the physical universe with human passions, while his tragedy itself was an attempt to moralise that religion and through it nature as a whole. Whence its superiority; for the moral illusion is, after all, that which stands the best chance of not being altogether false, and even if false, is still the most ennobling and sustaining. And this is just the character of a great literature everywhere, a profound conviction of the unreality of those

things which have been misnamed reality and
the substitution for them of some high and
abiding form of thought.

From our point of view, however, this moral
is, it must be added, of a peculiar sort. The
Greek, unlike the modern tragedian, made no
effort to deduce his *action* from character. In
this respect his drama is not moral, at least not
ethical at all. The essential matter for him
was not the manner in which personality is manifested in conduct. His first interest was in the
action itself. The persons were of subordinate
importance and derived their character, as well
as their significance, from the action. Aristotle
is explicit on this point. What principally
preoccupied the dramatist was the attempt to
justify the quality of good or evil with respect
to these actions as they tended to promote human happiness or the reverse. Were they pro-
ductive of misery, he had to demonstrate their
deviation from abstract right and justice, and
contrariwise. And so it is that in vindication
of the moral law the protagonist is always disposed of in accordance with the quality attached
to his acts, for, says Aristotle, "Men are so and
so by their characters, but happy or the reverse
by their actions." It is for this reason that the
Greek tragedies had such an exemplary force.
Since the *action* is not the outcome of a unique
character, but is only illustrated in the char-

acters, its like might occur to one person as well
as to another. Hence they touched the audience
with an immediacy of pity and horror to which
the romantic tragedy of character can make no
pretension. Hamlet's and Othello's fate can
befall only a Hamlet or an Othello; Œdipus'
and Orestes' might befall any one. Of course we
are bound to assume nowadays that nobody but
Œdipus could have behaved like Œdipus. But
not so the Greek; at all events that was not what
he undertook to show—the exclusively Orestean
nature of Orestes' deeds. His dramatic *motif*
affirmed only that the deeds were evil and
brought unhappiness, and were therefore to be
abhorred on the ground not merely of expediency
but of principle, while the character of Œdipus
or Orestes himself, who shared the obloquy of
the action, was revealed only in so far as it served
to support this conclusion. By the moral idea
of Greek tragedy, then, it is necessary to understand, not exactly an idea about human character and conduct in general, as Matthew Arnold
uses the term in his discussions of poetry, but
rather an idea about the quality of human actions, without particular reference to character,
in conformity with some abstract principle of
right and wrong.

To relieve this difference it is hardly necessary
to do more than compare the impressions to
which such plays as *Prometheus Bound, Œdipus*

Tyrannus, and *Iphigenia at Aulis* probably did once and certainly do now give rise. While we, untroubled for the moral consistency of our world, shudder at a suggestion of material confusion physical, social, or industrial, the great and haunting terror for the Greek, the nameless apprehension that lurked upon his life, stealing into consciousness at moments of depression and pervading the whole fabric of his tragic literature, was the dread of moral disorder. The horror of *Prometheus*, for instance, which has become for us, as far as the drama retains any meaning at all, a vague horror of chaos, of a world deranged or a lapse of "law," was undoubtedly to Æschylus exclusively moral. It was the horror of a profound and serious mind beginning to take account of its religious conceptions, its ideas of man and God, of guilt and responsibility, as contrasted with the horror of a present-day mind, accustomed to regard the stability of things as dependent upon the uniformity of nature rather than upon the integrity of the human spirit. To such a mind as was that of Æschylus, the story of Prometheus was a mystery, full of "labyrinths and meanders," unreasonable, monstrous, abhorrent, to be harmonised with the conscience at any cost. For with characteristic frankness the ancient dramatist recognised a set of "phenomena" whose significance we have now with characteristic

casuistry juggled away. I mean that kind of
case in which we have made a distinction as
between moral and physical consequences.
That there are occasions in this world when a
man is obliged to settle for debts which he has
neither incurred himself nor consented to, and
to expiate such consequences as he has never
foreseen, is undeniable. To our minds such
cases, though they continue to form the basis
of modern tragedy, are generally meaningless,
because we deny the victims' responsibility.
We are content with the air of baffling and in-
scrutable mystery which they diffuse about our
tragedy,

> dont les sombres pensées
> Sont d'un nuage épais toujours embarrassées,

and which indeed constitutes its prevailing tone.
But not so the Greek. With his moral prepossessions, with his tendency to see the moral everywhere, he was not willing to let such transactions
pass as irrelevant or meaningless or only mechan-
ically significant. They must, he felt, if the
moral consistency of the world was to be preserved, possess a moral import. And in such
case it was necessary to impute a moral account-
ability to their principals. Accordingly he never
thought of denying Prometheus' and Œdipus' responsibility. "῞Ημαρτον, οὐκ ἀρνήσομαι," says
Prometheus himself. Guilty without intention

even contrary *to* intention, they may have
been; but as human beings they were liable
for the consequences of their activity. And
while they were objects of pity on the one count,
they were as surely objects of horror on the other.
Hence the curious duplicity of feeling peculiar
to classic tragedy, which instinctively strikes
us, through our conventional admiration of antiquity, as gruesome and even shocking. And
indeed to us, in whose minds the moral illusion
is so greatly weakened, it seems no doubt a hard
saying that man is answerable for what he does
as well as for what he intends. We think to
enjoy the privilege of action without assuming the responsibility; and when anything
goes wrong, we have a convenient little way
of shrugging our shoulders and leaving it with
circumstance or providence. It is not so, however, that life would look to a consciousness
thoroughly and consistently moral. Such a
consciousness would find no satisfaction, either,
in a physiological interpretation of what was
and still is to some extent felt as the fatal obligation of blood, implicating the descendant in the
vices and virtues of his ancestors and making the
child responsible, like Iphigenia, for the parent;
for to such a consciousness the human creature
would appear, by the same illusion of moral
order, accountable for what it is as for what it
does. Nor is it wholly otiose in this connection

to refer to the exemplary "statue of Mitys at
Argos, which killed his murderer by falling upon
him while he was watching a spectacle"—a kind
of incident which appears to Aristotle highly
commendable for plots, "since such a thing
seems not to happen at random"; while to the
modern critic it looks altogether accidental and
quite unfit for tragedy, because where Aristotle
was ready to divine a judgment, and supply a
moral connection, we can detect only a bare
mechanical sequence without any retributive
force whatever. And so it is for this reason,
because we have shifted the centre of gravity
from man to nature, from the moral to the physical, that so much of modern tragedy is essentially fortuitous or unintelligible, or what comes
to the same thing, is spiritually irrelevant, a
tragedy

> Of accidental judgments, casual slaughters,

and that the classical tragedy has generally
turned to nonsense in the hands of its adapters.

To Corneille, for instance, Œdipus is merely
a blameless unfortunate. "[Il] me semble ne
faire aucune faute," he says. "bien qu'il tue
son père, parce qu'il ne le connoit pas et qu'il ne
fait que disputer le chemin en homme de cœur
contre un inconnu qui l'attaque avec avantage."
Hence his desperate and grotesque exertions
to put Œdipus obviously in the wrong, as he

succeeds in doing finally in a manner undreamed of by Sophocles, by hatching up a love affair detween Dirce and that universal lover Theseus, and making of Œdipus a commonplace and silly intermeddler. In like manner he professes himself unable to comprehend Sophocles' motive in prolonging the action of *Ajax* so far beyond the death of the protagonist; though with the assistance of Aristotle's commentary it ought to be clear enough that the quality of the action, the idea of the drama, remains undefined until the disposition of Ajax's body is finally settled. Indeed, Aristotle's whole teaching with regard to the characters and the "purgation of the passions" appears to him so dark, devious, and dangerous that, once having made it respectful obeisance, as to a Gessler's hat, he prudently takes another road for the future. Nor can Racine, who in imitating Euripides comes perhaps the nearest to imitating antiquity, see much more sense in Iphigenia, but attempts, with the aid of the unhappy and officious Eriphile to substitute a shabby and conventional poetic justice for the profound naturalism of the original fable. "Quelle apparence que j'eusse souillé la scene par le meutre d'une personne aussi aimable et aussi vertuese qu'il failloit représenter Iphigenie?" Even Euripides, who is himself, on one side of his literary being, nothing more than an adapter of Greek tragedy, has so

little appreciation of the morality of his predecessors that he tries to evade it, whenever he
can, by some puerile *ex machina* interference or
some decadent falsification of motives. On the
one hand the *dénouement* of his *Iphigenia in
Aulis* is in flat contradiction with the *morale*
of the remainder of the piece. The sacrifice is
accomplished at Iphigenia's exit; the effect is
produced already, and the effort to arrest it
later is absurdity. On the other hand, his Orestes is no longer the pathetic and terrible figure
of tradition and tragedy, Electra's brother,
Clytemnestra's son. He is a contemptible,
whining, besotted, epileptic parricide, at the
mercy of a faithless and uxorious poltroon—
a thoroughly Ibsenesque situation. He is already near the bottom; he has one step farther
to fall into Racine's semi-comic dupe of a vain
and jealous coquette. While as for Seneca's,
Dryden and Lee's, and Voltaire's parodies, what
can be said of them, save only that such is the
power of the tremendous old story that it is
still capable of stirring obscurely the depths
of our nature in spite of these marplots, whenever they will let the son of Laius himself upon
the stage? Even Boileau, the last great arbiter
of things classical, how unequal does even he
show himself to the greatness of his theme!

> Aussi pour nous charmer, la tragedie en pleurs
> D'Oedipe tout sanglant fit parler les douleurs,

D'Oreste parricide exprima les alarmes,
Et, pour nous divertir, nous arracha les larmes.

It is not unlikely that in trying to make this
point at all, I have overemphasised it. Such
matters do not bear forcing. But I have done
all I set out to do if I have made it clear that
Greek tragedy did not pretend to represent actuality or any such physical or mechanical system
as seems to us to be implied by actuality. On
the contrary, it undertook to represent a series
of sensations (the action) which should produce
upon the spectators a deceptive effect of reality,
but should, in fact, differ from it altogether in
being informed with a moral idea, such idea
constituting the writer's sense of the transaction.
It is on this account that a Greek play seems to
us so set and rigid. It is indeed in durance—
in durance to a principle more or less abstract.

III

And yet, in spite of all his fumbling, something of this constraint, of this ideal purposefulness of classic tragedy Corneille felt, and not
only felt but also succeeded in imitating and in
fastening so unshakably upon the neo-classic
drama that it is conceptually more nearly akin
to the Greek than is that of any other nation,
though neither he himself nor his immediate
successors had fully measured the spirit that

they were imitating. But while he often missed
the idea of the Greek, he was very susceptible
to its form. And it is undoubtedly true that
the depth and seriousness of Greek tragedy, if
not actually due to this cause, was at all events
greatly intensified by its concision, which was,
in turn, more or less accidental and a result
of its peculiar manner of development. There
was no room in Greek drama for a distracting
play of circumstance. Its very limitations, as
is not unusual in art, made its strength. The
chorus, which anchored it so firmly to a given
ground and held it so closely to a brief moment
of time, prevented it from straying away in
search of incident or from dissipating its substance in irrelevant sentiment. It could not
become epic, on the one hand, a mere scenic
chronicle of events, or lyric, on the other, an
excited outburst of purely individual feeling.
It was forced to remain a *genre tranché*. In its
brief compass it could deal only with the
moral issue or upshot of an action as denoted
in character.

Something of this focalisation, then, it is certain that Corneille saw and aimed at in adopting
the "unities," which represented to him, as to
the critics of his day, the structural merits of
classicism. With regard to two of these unities,
those of time and place, it is fitting that a word
should be said. They have been so abused and

decried in the course of a long and violent reaction that they have finally come to appear something monstrous and abhorrent, a damning evidence of literary servility and fatuity. That they sometimes put Corneille and his followers to strange shifts can not be gainsaid. But the fault was not so much theirs as the dramatists', who were frequently unwilling to accept a stuff, or unable to cast it into a shape conformable with their own theories.

It has been generally assumed that the unities of time and place were only devices for securing verisimilitude. And inasmuch as it is indifferently easy for their enemies to show that they contribute nothing to the probability of drama, but quite the contrary, and as their friends with singular blindness have insisted upon defending them on grounds so obviously false and untenable, the romanticists have leaped to the conclusion that they are altogether vain and inadmissible on any grounds. The fact is, however, that to Corneille, as to all the neo-classicists, whether they were conscious of it or not, the unities of time and place were, in actual practice, nothing more than a convention to secure dramatic relevancy and concentration. In this respect they were quite successful and were used by Shakespeare in *Othello* and by Æschylus in *Agamemnon* and the *Eumenides*, to mention but a few instances, although it was

Corneille who first reduced them to a regular theatrical *procédé* in taking them up into his drama and reinforcing them in his *Examens* and *Discours* with an ample apologetic criticism. With this assistance it is by no means difficult to follow the steps by which the convention was developed or to define the exact shape which it finally took to his imagination.

In the *Cid* he is as yet rather embarrassed. He acknowledges as much in the *Examen:* that he has managed matters rather clumsily and that he did not then see his way clear to the manner in which the unity of time might be made a practicable working stage device. Indeed it is doubtful whether he had as yet divined the ideal to which such a unity would contribute. But it did not take him long to perceive that the reckoning of dramatic time is at best a very uncertain process; and consequently, when events are sown thickly together, without any reference to their duration, the impression produced is as likely to be that of a day as of any other period. In other words, he understood what dramatists have always understood and critics have often forgotten, that a play is meant to be acted and seen, not pored over and anatomised, and that dramatic effect is largely an affair of hints, suggestions, and intimations, to which the audience pays small attention at the moment but which produce their result insensi-

bly and in the mass. And therefore it is no
very difficult matter to crowd the stage with
incidents in a manner quite impossible to the
reason, and yet to give the impression that they
are confined to twenty-four hours in the natural-
est way in the world.   In short, it is an affair of
plausibility, not of probability.   And this is virtually Corneille's discovery—a discovery which
made the unity of time possible as a condition
of French tragedy.

Il est si malaisé qu'il se rencontre, dans l'histoire ny
dans l'imagination des hommes, quantité de ces événe-
mens illustres et dignes de la tragédie, dont les délibér-
ations et leurs effets puissent arriver en un mesme lieu
et en un mesme jour sans faire un peu de violence à
l'ordre commun des choses, que je ne puis croire cette
sorte de violence tout à fait condamnable, pourveu
qu'elle n'aille pas jusqu'à l'impossible.   Il est de beaux
sujets où on ne la peut éviter, et un autheur scrupuleux
se priveroit d'une belle occasion, et le public de beaucoup de satisfaction, s'il n'osoit s'enhardir à les mettre
sur le théatre, de peur de se voir forcé à les faire aller
plus viste que le vray-semblance ne le permet.   Je luy
donneroit, en ce cas, un conseil que peut-estre il trouve-
roit salutaire : c'est de ne marquer aucun temps préfix
dans son poëme, ny aucun lieu determiné où il pose ses
acteurs.   L'imagination de l'auditeur auroit plus de
liberté de se laisser aller au courant de l'action si elle
n'étoit point fixée par ces marques, et il pourroit ne
s'appercevoir de cette précipitation, si elles ne l'en
faisoient souvenir et n'y appliquoient son esprit malgré
luy.

As for the unity of place he would treat that

in general like the unity of time; he would, that
is, allow himself, to begin with, as much latitude
as he could plausibly neutralise in the final effect produced upon the audience. Between the
treatment of time and place in drama, however,
there is unfortunately one serious difference.
In the case of the former there is nothing in the
nature of a play that need remind the spectators
of the duration of the action as such; whereas
the *mise en scène*, the scenery and stage-setting,
forces the latter consideration immediately upon
the attention of the audience. The only way
out of the difficulty would seem to consist in
making the setting as non-committal as possible
and in particular in avoiding all changes of
scenery, whether the action shifts its ground
or not, just as all indications of time were pre-
viously avoided.

Je tiens donc qu'il faut chercher cette unité exacte
autant qu'il est possible; mais comme elle ne s'accom-
mode pas avec toute sorte de sujets, j'accorderois tres-
volontiers que ce qu'on feroit passer en une seule ville
auroit l'unité de lieu. Ce n'est pas que je volusse que
le théatre representast cette ville toute entiére (cela
seroit un peu trop vaste), mais seulement deux ou trois
lieux particuliers enfermez dans l'enclos de ses mu-
railles. . . . Pour rectifier en quelque façon cette
duplicité de lieu quand elle est inévitable, je voudrois
qu'on fist deux choses: l'une que jamais on ne changeast
dans le mesme acte, mais seulement de l'un à l'autre,
comme il se fait dans les trois prémiers de *Cinna;*
l'autre, que ces deux lieux n'eussent point besoin de

diverses décorations, et qu'aucun des deux ne fust jamais nommé, mais seulement le lieu général où tous les deux sont compris, comme Paris, Rome, Lyon, Constantinople, etc. Cela aideroit à tromper l'auditeur, qui, ne voyant rien qui luy marquast la diversité des lieux, ne s'en appercevroit pas, à moins d'une reflexion malicieuse et critique, dont il y en a peu qui soient capable, la pluspart s'attachant avec chaleur à l'action qu'ils voyent representer.

That is to say, if the stage represent no place in particular, or represent a place with no particular character, there will be no remarkable incongruity in seeing any or all of the characters appear in such a scene, for it is obviously the kind of place in which any one might appear, though there is, to be sure, no particular reason that any one in particular should appear there. Such a place would naturally be a room,—an out-door scene would be too characteristic and peculiar for the purpose; and it would be a public room of some sort, or certain of the characters might seem out of place or suggest awkward doubts of their motives. So in the *Examen* of *Polyeucte*:

L'autre scrupule regarde l'unité du lieu, qui est assez exacte, puisque tout s'y passe dans une salle ou antichambre commune aux apartemens de Félix et sa fille. Il semble que la bien-séance y soit un peu forcée pour conserver cette unité au second acte, en ce que Pauline vient jusque dans cette antichambre pour trouver Sévére, dont elle devroit attendre la visite dans son cabinet. A quoy je répons qu'elle a eu deux raisons de venir au devant de luy: l'une pour faire plus d'honneur à un homme dont son père redoutoit l'indignation, et qu'il luy avoit commandé d'adoucir en sa faveur; l'autre, pour rompre plus aisément la conversation avec luy, en se retirant dans ce cabinet, s'il ne vouloit pas la quitter à son priére et se délivrer par cette retraite d'un entretien dangereux pour celle, ce qu'elle n'eust pû faire si elle eust receu sa visite dans son apartement.

This is the second stage. The apologetic ingenuity is misplaced and weakens the case by continuing to rest it on the mistaken principle of verisimilitude. He should have claimed at the very outset the immunity of convention—just as he goes on to do a little later when he comes to understand the real strength of his position and pushes his idea to a logical conclusion.

In order that a play may go on it is necessary that the characters meet. Now, inasmuch as the characters are represented by the actors, these characters will appear to meet whenever the actors do. But the actors meet on the stage, and the stage is decorated to represent a scene. The difference between the stage and a scene, however, consists in this, that the one belongs to the theatrical reality, the other to the dramatic fiction; so that the scenery transforms the stage into an imaginary realm supposedly within the bounds of the play. Of course this is just the difficulty. But it may be obviated by letting the decoration represent a public room, as before, but one which all the characters

are free to enter under any circumstances, avowedly on some more or less probable pretext, but
in reality and by tacit agreement for the sake
of carrying on the piece.

Mais, comme les personnes qui ont des intérests
opposez ne peuvent pas vray-semblablement expliquer
leurs secrets en mesme place, et qu'ils sont quelquefois
introduits dans le mesme acte, avec liaison de scénes
qui emportent nécessairement cette unité, il faut trouver un moyen qui la rende compatible avec cette contradiction qu'y forme la vray-semblance rigoreuse. . . .
Les jurisconsultes admettent des fictions de droit, et
je voudrois, à leur example, introduire des fictions de
théatre pour établir un lieu théatral qui ne seroit ny
l'apartement de Cléopatre, ny celuy de Rodogune dans
la piéce qui porte ce tître, ny celuy de Phocas, de
Léontine, ou de Pulchérie dans *Héraclius*, mais une
salle sur laquelle ouvrent ces divers apartemens, à qui
j'attribuërois deux priviléges: l'un, que chacun de ceux
qui y parleroient fust présumé y parler avec le mesme
secret que s'il étoit dans sa chambre; l'autre, qu'au
lieu que dans l'ordre commun il est quelquefois de
la bienséance que ceux qui occupent le théatre aillent
trouver ceux qui sont dans leur cabinet pour parler à
eux, ceux-cy pûssent les venir trouver sur le théatre
sans choquer cette bienséance, afin de conserver l'unité
de lieu et la liaison des scénes.

It is easy enough to say that this is conventional and artificial; but that once said, the worst
is over.   To be sure, in such a practice time and
place were abstract.   But the statement means
nothing more than that they belonged to the
play, not to reality; that they pertained to the

idea of the *genre*, not to the idea of nature—
which is no more than to say that a play is a
play. Or, to put it in other words, the drama
happened on the stage for as long as it was acting—surely no very grave fault in a stage play,
since everybody knows that it never happened
elsewhere or at any other time. Schlegel himself states the principle clearly enough in his
Dramatische Kunst und Litteratur, though he
misapplies it mischievously:

Der Begriff der Taüschung hat in der Kunsttheorie
grosse Irrungen angerichtet. Man hat oft darunter
den unwilkürlich gewordenen Irrthum verstanden, als
ob das Dargestellte wirklich sey. . . . Nein, die thea-
tralische Taüschung wie jede poetische ist eine wache
Traümerey, des man sich freywillig hingiebt. Um sie
hervorzubringen, müssen Dichter und Schauspieler
die Gemüther lebhaft hinreissen, die berechneten Wahr-
scheinlichkeiten helfen nicht im mindesten dazu.

Exactly: the illusion of art—and the wonder is
that any one should forget it—is wholly specious.
Such was the spirit of Corneille's teaching.
And judiciously managed in accordance with
this spirit, as Racine finally caught the trick of
managing them, the unities of time and place
are in themselves no more shocking than the
gross conventions of the Elizabethan stage, for
which we show ourselves so tender because they
happen to be in our way—a placard doing duty
for a scene or a lantern for the moon or other

such like clumsy makeshifts as Shakespeare has himself ridiculed in the *Midsummer Night's Dream*. But, to push the case at once to an extreme, is the fact that the action of *Bérénice*, after the fashion of *Polyeucte*, passes willy-nilly in an ante-chamber contiguous to the apartments of Titus and Bérénice any more offensive to "verisimilitude" than the chasm between the third and fourth acts of the *Winter's Tale?*⁎ The fact is that Corneille and Racine may be right as well as Shakespeare. For as long as the main business of drama is accomplished, what difference does it make about such matters as these? Given the type of tragedy, it is of very small moment, after all, where *Bérénice* takes place, provided only the display of emotion for whose sake the piece exists be adequately carried off. In the whole range of neo-classic tragedy, it is safe to say, there is no more audacious violation of probability, no more purely artificial device, than the "double time," so called, which gives rapidity and intensity to *Othello*. If it is improbable that Titus and Bérénice should in reality open their hearts so freely as they do in the place assigned them, it is physically impossible, not to say absolutely inconceivable, that Desdemona should deceive her husband in the time at her disposal. If Othello could have told the hours, the murder would never have been committed. And what is so singular, in the light of that romantic criticism which is continually reproaching Racine with Shakespeare, is the fact that the Shakespearean contrivance is in this case of exactly the same character as that by virtue of which Corneille begins by cramming the events of the *Cid* into a single day—what else is it than a unity of time?—only more daring. Nor does Æschylus do otherwise in making the return of Agamemnon succeed immediately upon the fall of Troy; it is but one time and one scene. Beside such examples the procedures of Racine and Corneille, which we are invited to reprobate as unnatural, are marvels of verisimilitude and credibility. So true is it that Shakespeare himself, or any other playwright for that matter, had no slightest compunction in using a bold and literally impossible artifice when it suited his purpose. What cared he, or Æschylus, in such a case for a timorous probability as long as he secured the dramatic intensity which the play demanded? Indeed, as Shakespeare proves —even to the satisfaction of the romanticists, I hope—such artifices are as likely to help as hinder; it all lies in their appropriateness. So the bare stage was an advantage to the romantic drama, whose strength consisted in reproducing, by a variety of incident, a sense of the bewildering *wirr-warr* of existence. And equally was the rigidity of the performance an advantage

to Greek tragedy, whose strength consisted in
the illustration of moral ideas.   The only question, then, is not whether such a device is conventional and artificial, but is it in harmony with
the spirit of the drama to which it is applied
and does it assist the impression which that
drama aims to produce?   Only, if there is to be
a convention, let it be as simple and elementary
as possible.   A monologue, for instance, is better
than a "confidant" male or female, a direct ex-
planatory address to the audience in the Greek
manner than such an exposition as introduces
Voltaire's *Oedipe* or Corneille's *Medée*.

> J'aimerois mieux encore qu'il declinast son nom,
> Et dit: "Je suis Oreste," ou bien "Agamemnon."

But while the neo-classicists were by no means
blameless in these respects, yet the unities of
time and place did, on the whole, agree so thoroughly with the general intent of their tragedy
that it remains, with all its faults, the strongest
structurally and the most effectual in design—
that is, the most responsive to ideas—of any
modern tragedy: so false is the whole romantic
working-hypothesis that lawlessness is strength.

IV

And yet there were dangers which neither
Corneille nor his successors escaped in attempting to reproduce the formal austerity of Greek

tragedy. For if the unities of time and place have their conveniency, they have their liabilities, too; and it would have been well if their employers had always remembered that, while they were favourable to a strictly ideal design, they were altogether incompatible with breadth and variety of action or theatrical exuberance of any kind. Racine puts the matter very clearly in the preface to *Bérénice*.

Mais ce qui m'en plût davantage, c'est que je le [le sujet] trouvai extrêmement simple. [And he continues:] Il n'y a que le vraysemblance qui touche dans le tragédie, et quelle vraysemblance y a-t-il qu'il arrive en un jour une multitude de choses qui pourroient à peine arriver en plusieurs semaines? Il y en a qui pensent que cette simplicité est une marque de peu d'invention. Ils ne songent pas qu'au contraire toute l'invention consiste à faire quelque chose de rien, et que tout ce grand nombre d'incidents a toujours esté le refuge des poëtes qui ne sentoient dans leur genie ni assez d'abondance ni assez de force pour attacher durant cinq actes leurs spectateurs par *une action simple, soutenuë de la violence des passions, de la beauté des sentimens, et de l'élegance de l'expression.*

This is undoubtedly the formula of such a type of drama, not on account of "*vraysemblance*," wherewith we still love to delude ourselves, but on account of artistic consistency, which would preclude the use of a form for any other purpose than that for which it is fitted. And to this law, the law of congruous simplicity,

Racine conforms pretty faithfully. Both Corneille and Voltaire, however, are grave offenders; and though Corneille's superiority as a dramatist is so great that he carries it off very much better than Voltaire, yet even his plays do not escape the sort of grotesqueness which arises from the application of a simple and severe method to a luxurious and diversified material. No one has ever felt the effect of the inconsistency more keenly, though he seems to have no suspicion of the cause of it. Hear him discoursing of the four last scenes of the first act of the *Cid;* it is one of the curiosities of literature :

> Le Comte et D. Diégue se querellent au sortir du palais: cela peut passer dans une rue; mais après la soufflet receu, D. Diégue ne peut pas demeurer dans cette rue à faire ses plaintes, attendant que son fils survienne, qu'il ne soit tout aussitot environné de peuple et ne recoive l'offre de quelques amis. . . . En l'état où elles [les scènes] sont icy, on peut dire qu'il faut quelquefois aider au théatre, et suppléer favorablement ce qui ne s'y peut representer. . . . Ainsi, par une fiction de théatre, on peut s'imaginer que D. Diégue et le Comte, sortant du palais du Roy, avancent toujours en se querellant et sont arrivez devant le maison de ce prémier, lors qu'il reçoit le soufflet, qui l'oblige à y entrer pour y chercher du secours.

And all this in spite of the fact that the Count and Don Diégue move not at all and that the scenery never changes. It was this sort of thing which provoked Dryden to remark facetiously

that in regular French drama "the street, the
window, the houses, the closet, are made to walk
about, and the persons to stand still." But the
cream of Corneille's commentary remains:

> Si cette fiction poétique ne vous satisfait point, lais-
> sons le [D. Diégue] dans la place publique, et disons
> que le concours de peuple autour de luy, aprés cette
> offense, et les offres que luy font les prémiers amis qui
> s'y rencontrent, sont des circonstances que le roman ne
> doit pas oublier, mais que, ces menuës actions ne ser-
> vant de rien à la principale, il n'est pas besoin que le
> poëte s'en embarasse sur la scéne.

Such is the desperate plight to which Corneille
is reduced in his first masterpiece in order to
give a kind of plausibility to its successive
scenes. And though it must be remembered
that the *Cid* is one of his freer plays, and that
his comments with respect to it are intended
to be apologetic rather than exemplary, yet the
case, while an extreme, is withal a fair one. In
almost every instance Corneille's intrigue is too
complicated for his form. His *Rodogune*, for
instance, on which he prided himself particularly,
is on this account curious rather than impressive; and the "inventiveness" of the fifth act,
which Voltaire pretended to admire and tried
to imitate, with even worse effect, is, under the
circumstances, a blemish rather than a beauty.
Indeed, he as much as confesses the fault himself, and even prides himself upon it with an

ingenious and amusing vainglory quite his own.
Of *Heraclius* he remarks justly enough:

> . . . Le poëme est si embarrassé qu'il demande une
> marveilleuse attention. J'ay veu de fort bons es-
> prits, et des personnes des plus qualifiées de la Cour,
> se plaindre de ce que sa représentation fatiguoit au-
> tant l'esprit qu'une étude sérieuse. Elle n'a pas laissé
> de plaire, mais je croy qu'il l'a fallu voir plus d'une
> fois pour en remporter une entiére intelligence.

In short, Corneille is romantic by his plot and
classic by his design. And it is to this fundamental incongruity between the form and the
fond of his drama that his difficulties with the
unities and his frequent apologies are due.

Nor is the tendency to stuff the action the
only lee shore upon which neo-classicism drifted
in attempting to lay its course by Aristotle and
the Greek tragedians. It was all very well to
attempt to bring the French drama out of the
maelstrom of romanticism and to devote it to
the service of ideas, provided the dramatist had
any ideas to devote it to. But inasmuch as the
unities rigidly limited the amount of incident,
reducing the action almost to the dimensions
of a situation as compared with that of the romantic drama, this very limitation was liable,
in default of any serious or worthy purpose, to
leave the writer, like Benvenuto Cellini, without
sufficient materials for his casting, and oblige
him to an unnatural prolongation of the action,

particularly as the modern taste demanded a
larger play than the ancient. In short, in assuming the restrictions which would assist in
the expression of a genuine idea, the dramatist,
in the absence of such an idea or in case of its
inadequacy, ran the risk of falling into a sort
of casuistical extenuation of what motives,
emotions, and the like the situation afforded him,
eking them out as best he could with aphorisms,
sententiæ, gnomic utterances, commonplaces, and
what not, which lent an air of factitious moral
reflection to his drama. To read Corneille in
one mood it would seem as though the *Cid* must
have attracted him, as it might have attracted
Dryden, for the equivocalness of the situations;
for there is nothing more common in literature
than the acquirement of a taste for what was
originally a defect and the gradual erection of
a failing into a merit and a subject of imitation.
Certainly in such speeches as Chiméne's,

> Pour conserver ma gloire et finir mon ennuy,
> Le poursuivre, le prendre, et mourir après luy,
> *Le Cid*, iii., 3.

the dramatist is swimming triumphantly in some
supersensible medium, equally remote from the
idealised atmosphere of the Greek and the romantic æther of Shakespeare—the kind of medium which characterises such plays as the
Conquest of Granada or *Aureng-Zebe*. So too in

Horace—to set aside pieces like *Heraclius* in which the *equivoque* is inherent in the material— the permutations and combinations of relationship and of feeling between Camille, Sabine, Horace, and Curiace are figured out, not only with amazing thoroughness and ingenuity, but also with something of that forced and factitious wit which is nowadays associated with the name of Cowley. Nor, in fact, is Corneille, like Cowley, without a weakness for quibbles even in the most inappropriate places. While the elder Horace is bewailing what he supposes to be the cowardice of his surviving son fleeing before the Curiaces, he has still levity enough to excogitate his little witticism.

> N'eust-il que d'un moment reculé sa defaite,
> Rome eust été du moins un peu plus tard sujette.
> *Horace*, iii., 6.

But the fourth and fifth scenes of this same act, the third, are the triumph of that sort of emotional emulation or competition of sensibility which makes this literature look at times like a mere work of ingenuity—an attempt to see how many changes might be rung upon a given theme.[1]

---

[1] For some suggestive remarks on the character and result of Corneille's dramatic casuistry, consult Brunetière's *Études critiques sur l'historie de la Littérature française*, vi., Corneille, sec. ii.

Nor for all his tact is Racine by any means
innocent of the same vice. The passage in which
Aricie undertakes to explain her love for Hippo-
lytus, though well known, is too good an example
to remain unquoted:

> J'aime, je l'avoûray, cet orgueil genereux
> Qui jamais n'a fleché sous le joug amoureux.
> Phedre en vain s'honoroit des soupirs de Thesée:
> Pour moy, je suis plus fière, et fuis la gloire aisée
> D'arracher un hommage à mille autres offert,
> Et d'entrer dans un cœur de toutes parts ouvert.
> Mais de faire flechir un courage inflexible,
> De porter la douleur dans une ame insensible,
> D'enchaîner un captif de ses fers étonné,
> Contre un joug qui luy plaist vainement mutiné:
> C'est la ce que je veux, c'est la ce qui m'irrite,
> Hercule à desarmer coûtoit moins qu'Hippolyte,
> Et, vaincu plus souvent, et plûtost surmonté,
> Preparoit moins de gloire aux yeux qui l'ont donté.
>
> *Phedre*, ii., 1.

This is not to exhibit human character or passion, to say nothing of human action; it is merely
to force an opportunity, to exploit a situation.
And, though it is necessary to forgive much to an
episode which serves as an occasion to Phedre's
magnificent outburst of jealousy in the closing
scene of the fourth act, the weakness of such a
passage is unmistakable.

With Racine and Corneille the drama is indeed something more than this. With Voltaire,
however, it is just about this and little more. It

is very much with respect to action what a pun
is with respect to language, a play upon incidents, a dramatic quibble—a fact which may
account for the inveteracy with which he praises
Horace in and out of season.

Chere Obeide!

exclaims the condemned lover in the *Scythes*,

> Prends ce fer, ne crains rien; que ton bras homicide
> Frappe un cœur à toi seule en tout temps reservé;
> On y verra ton nom; c'est la qu'il est gravé.
> *Les Scythes*, v., 5.

Even Goethe himself, when he attempts to be
classical, does not escape. His *Iphigenie* is
neither the expression of characters in action nor
the notation of a transaction by means of characters.   It contains neither actions nor passions.
It is rather the protraction of a situation in ": sentences"; and however noble and elevated those
sentences, it has very much the same air of research which has perhaps done more than anything else to give this whole literature the name
of "artificial."

And yet this subtilisation of motives, particularly those of a paradoxical or antithetical sort,
conveys a suggestive and instructive lesson;
because the weakness would seem to be, not
merely coincident with a certain school or period,
but inevitable whenever the modern attempts
to revive the spirit of antiquity, as though to

us its singleness of eye, its grave and congruous
simplicity were forever impossible—this curious
dialectic and a peculiar sort of flatness or tepidity
which is the natural counterpart of such an ingenuity and which is so familiar to every reader
of French poetry. Without going outside the
language compare, for example, this morsel of
Corneille's *Suite du Menteur*, which Voltaire
singles out for special praise, with a brief passage
from a writer who, himself an admirer of the
ancients, was yet quite untouched by the classical literary affectation, the artistry, of the renaissance—I mean Montaigne:

Quand les ordres du Ciel nous ont fait l'un pour l'autre,
Lyse, c'est un accord bien tost fait que le nostre.
Sa main entre les cœurs, par un secret pouvoir,
Séme l'intelligence avant que de se voir;
Il prépare si bien l'amant et la maîtresse
Que leur âme au seul nom s'emeut et s'intéresse:
On s'estime, on se cherche, on s'aime en un moment;
Tout ce qu'on s'entredit persuade aisément,
Et, sans s'inquiéter d'aucunes peurs frivoles,
Le foy semble courir au devant des paroles.
La langue en peu de mots en explique beaucoup;
Les yeux, plus éloquens, font tout voir tout d'un coup;
Et, de quoy qu'à l'envy tous les deux nous s'instruisent,
Le cœur en entend plus que tous les deux n'en disent.
                                    La Suite du Menteur, iv., 1.

It is on a somewhat similar subject, his friend-
ship for de la Boëtie, that Montaigne speaks in
the following terms:

Si l'on me presse de dire pourquoy je l'aymois, je sens
que cela ne se peut exprimer: il y a, ce semble, au delà
de tout mon discours et de ce que j'en puis dire, ne sçay
quelle force divine et fatale, mediatrice de cette union.
Ce n'est pas une particuliere consideration, ny deux, ny
trois, ny quatre, ny mille; c'est je ne sçay quelle quinte
essence de tout ce meslange, qui, ayant saisi toute ma
volonté, l'amena se plonger et se perdre dans la sienne.
Je dis perdre, à la verité, ne luy reservant rien qui luy
fust propre ny qui fust sien.

It seems, indeed, as though there were but a
single moment in the world's history when men
could be unaffectedly simple without shallowness or banality; and, that moment passed, they
must needs be intricate or nothing.

Les grandes choses, says Sainte-Beuve, et qui sont
simples à la fois, ont été dites de bonne heure: les an-
ciens moralistes et poëtes ont dessiné et saisi la nature humaine dans ses principaux et larges traits; il
semble qu'ils n'aient laissé aux modernes que la décou-
verte des détails et la grâce des raffinements.

And so, if the inference is correct, it evidently
indicates a source of weakness as dangerous to
modern classicism as is the risk of distraction
and confusion to romanticism.

L'esclave imitateur nâit et s'évanouit;
La nuit vient, le corps reste, et son ombre s'en-
fuit.

ANATOLE FRANCE

LATE as was Anatole France to assume the role of reviewer, there were early noticeable in his novels an air of half-humorous, half-ironical detachment from the more active interests of life, a disposition to general ideas, and a curious sublimation of thought which brought them nearer to criticism, especially criticism after his own kind, than the novel usually dares to steer. It was fiction of a new sort—fiction drenched with ideas to the point of saturation; and if it is the office of criticism to elicit ideas and hold them up to contemplation, then in so far it was already criticism too. And yet, amply endowed in this vein as their writer would seem to have been, it must be confessed that after his novels his reviews, of which there are four volumes now collected, come as something of a disappointment. They are delightful reading as far as they go; but they are tantalisingly brief—altogether too short to accommodate the plenary amplitude of critical development, which is bound by its nature to be discursive if it is to be effective; while, delightful as they are singly, it is impossible to read many of them without becoming conscious of the trick—the

251

kind of sentimental heightening or magnification which the author applies to all subjects regardless of their relative merits or importance. Of method or system his criticism is, indeed, guiltless; but this *procédé*, this aggrandisement of every topic indiscriminately by exploiting its personal interest or relation to the writer, soon becomes unpleasantly conspicuous. On the whole, then, the most interesting portions of the collection are the prefaces to the several volumes, in which he undertakes to set out a consecutive account of his idea and practice of criticism.

Anatole France is a critic, so he would have us believe, very much as Sedaine was a poet—for fun, *pour rire*. "I am no critic at all," he declares in his pleasant airy way; "I should n't know how to manage the threshing-machine into which clever persons throw the literary harvest to separate the wheat from the chaff. If literature has stories as the fairies have, then these are of them." In this spirit of modest deprecation he goes on to disclaim, for himself in particular and for the critic in general, all title to the ancient traditional rights and properties of criticism, especially those of judgment and authority.

Criticism, he confesses with cheerful alacrity, is a sort of novel for the use of advised and curious spirits. And as every novel, properly understood, is an autobiography, the good critic is one who relates his adventures with masterpieces. [Here one might inquire, parenthetically, if criticism is all a matter of personal liking, why, then, should the critic be restricted to masterpieces, and if so, how are these masterpieces to be decided upon?] There is no more an objective criticism, he continues, than there is an objective art; and all those who flatter themselves on putting anything other than themselves into their work are dupes of the most fallacious sort of illusion. The truth is, one can never get outside of oneself. That is our greatest misfortune. What would n't we give to see heaven and earth for a moment with the faceted eye of the fly, or to comprehend nature with the rude and simple brain of the orang-outang? But that is forbidden us. We can not, like Teresias, be a man and remember how it seemed to be a woman. We are each enclosed in his own person as in a perpetual prison. The best we can do, it seems to me, is to recognise this frightful condition of things with good grace and confess that we are talking about ourselves every time we are weak enough to talk at all.

Now this is all very sprightly, very brilliant, and very entertaining indeed. And it is on the strength of these, his own protestations, that Anatole France has come to be reputed the critic of caprice, of mere personal inclination, and to be lauded, it must be confessed, by many of the lighter-minded who would have been the first to decry the very same work had it been offered them with a solemn countenance. But one acquainted with Renan, the spirit from whom Anatole France most derives, may be permitted to doubt the absolute sincerity of these professions. If there is anything these gentlemen love, it is some such little mystification as this, some such innocent little assumption of indifference to the sterner aspects of things. They are so modestly self-conscious that they dread to appear too much in earnest; and, in order to shield themselves from the ridicule of those less really serious than themselves, they have recourse to all sorts of guileless little artifices—they are quizzical and paradoxical, in their moments of desperation they even go the length of denying their own virtues. In this strain M. France pretends that artlessness is his only skill, artlessness and the inability to conceal his failings—he, the author of *la Rôtisserie de la Reine Pédauque*, the most subtle and malicious spirit of our times! Indeed, it is just this mixture of malice and subtlety which makes the seduction of all his books, criticism and fiction alike. Under these circumstances, then, we may be forgiven, in seeking to escape for once being any one's dupe but our own, if we prefer to lean for our opinion rather upon our author's work than upon his representations of that work.

The fact is that M. France has very nimbly dodged the point. The question, after all, is not whether criticism is subjective or objective, personal or impersonal, since the relativity of things human is indisputable, and it will not be denied, I suppose, that criticism, in spite of

M. Brunetière, is human still. But, what is very
different, the real, the vital question is whether
criticism is a matter of caprice or principle.
Morality, for instance, is certainly personal and
subjective, and may vary with individuals and
circumstances, no hard and fast rule fitting every
instance.   But at the same time the essential
is, not that our codes should all concur, if only
they are capable of sustaining a fair examination
and justifying themselves for their possessors
before reasonable beings; that is, if they are only
grounded on considerations broader than the
mere instinct of any one particular case.   A
man who acts consistently by the application
of such a code we call a man of principle, and
justly so, though his conduct may differ widely
under similar circumstances from another's
whose principles are equally sound.   And the
same thing is true, I venture to think, of criticism. It is not necessary, or even desirable, that
every one of us, diverse as we are, should adjudge
every literary matter in precisely the same way;
but it is desirable and necessary, as actually
happens with most of us consciously or unconsciously, that we adjudge such matters
on grounds which, if exhibited, would compel
general appreciation and respect, though not
necessarily general acceptance or imitation.

One of the most curious experiences of the
literary life is the quarrel which occasionally

arises in the reader's mind between his inclination and his conscience. Every one who has
read at all has probably felt himself divided
some time or other, if but for a moment, between
what he likes and what he feels that he ought to
like—has recognised at least the inferiority of
the book he chose for the nonce to that other
which for the nonce he laid aside. "The books
that we reread the oftenest are not always those
that we admire the most," says Stevenson; and
it will not be gainsaid that Stevenson has given
satisfactory evidence to the possession both of
literary conscience and of literary whim. Of
the fact itself various explanations may be
offered. It is possible that one book satisfies an
appetite particularly exigent at the moment; one
amuses while another instructs. Or very likely
the book felt as superior requires for its enjoyment an elevation of faculty impossible at the
time. But, however that may be, the significant
matter is that we recognise the distinction, and
recognising it against our immediate inclination,
must do so by virtue of some broader, more
general consideration—that is, by virtue of a
principle.

Of course it is impossible to know whether
Anatole France has reckoned in these items in
making up his accounts with criticism. He may
be one of those happily constituted natures
whose desires are always just what they should

be, so that he is unconscious of any such unfortunate dispute, as Renan would express it,
among the lobes of his brain. But it is hard to
believe that one so acute should have overlooked
even so small a bit of evidence or failed to draw
the inevitable conclusion, particularly when his
criticism itself is found to proceed, albeit so
airily, on a tacit recognition of the truth involved.
The philosophy that underlies his work may not
be formally systematised—all the better for the
purpose if it is not, if it is still fluid enough to
adapt itself to all the sinuosities of its subject;
but that a philosophy of some sort does broadly
underlie and support his work, no one who
has read it understandingly can doubt. The
"natural love for the good and the beautiful"
which he professes and his avowed preference
for the masterpiece are both tenets of an un-
written creed—to say nothing of the position
which he has just been seen to take in his prefaces; for if there is one philosophy more positive than another it is that which asserts the
vanity of positive convictions.

But something more is wanting to set M.
France's criticism in the right light. Whatever
its failings in profession, as a protest against the
constantly growing tendency to reduce literature to the denominations of science, particularly
of psychology and sociology, it is as commendable as it is just. Indeed it is not improbably

17

in the violence of his reaction to this tendency that he has suffered himself to be carried so far in the opposite direction—farther than he would else have gone. But be that as it may, he has recognised with unerring perspicacity, for all the confusion about him, that such attempts are as impertinent and abortive as the effort to square the circle or the search for the philosopher's stone, and betray as common an ignorance of the very nature of the subject. "What science seeks after," Matthew Arnold very broadly observes, "is a satisfying rational conception of things." And in this one general sense, perhaps, criticism may be called "scientific," if one wish, since it does seek after "a satisfying rational conception" of its own affairs in its own way. But if by "scientific" be meant the application to literary matters of the methods of some particular positive science, then indeed criticism never will and never can be scientific. Criticism has its own method adapted to its own ends, to which it is hardly reasonable to object because it is not some other method; for by such a logic what would become of the methods of psychology and sociology themselves as tried by mathematics and physics? Is there not something infinitely amusing in the assurance with which these two former sciences, as they love to call themselves, insist upon upbraiding criticism for its dissoluteness and proposing to reform its

habits? The psychologist or sociologist who
tries to comprehend the product of genius in his
airless formulæ, may possibly be doing a very useful work; but he must not imagine for a moment
that his work has anything in particular to do
with literature. Who can read the ingenious
M. Hennequin, for instance, without being
perfectly conscious that he is writing about
something very interesting, very important, no
doubt, but quite irrelevant to criticism? The
scholar, as the word is used to-day, and the critic
are not only speaking two different languages;
they are talking about two different things.
Literature is intelligible only in its own tongue;
its essence escapes in translation. He who
would criticise a poem must be himself a poet;
and his criticism, to fit his subject, must be as
elastic and pliant as a lady's glove.

Obviously there can be no science of literature,
no "scientific criticism," until there is a science
of life. But life is licentious. Let us acknowledge it courageously; whatever life may be
absolutely, it is within the narrow limits of
human consciousness irrational and unprognosticable,—it is, as we say, lawless. And if in
a work of art there exists an order, a regularity,
a rhythm, it exists not in virtue of a law but in
virtue of the arbitrary and unaccountable
discriminations of an individual temperament.
It is a matter of selection and arrangement in the

interests of a sentiment or impression, which is, in its turn, from the point of view of science, irrational and unprognosticable and lawless. For the principle as well as the substance of literature is the disturbing element of science, "the factor of error," which under the name of "personal equation" the latter seeks to eliminate as far as it can. In short, either one of these alternatives must be true: either science, in attempting to reduce literature to its tributary, is guilty of a gross absurdity, an egregious confusion of terms; or else in the general laxity of modern thought the idea of science, like almost all our other ideas, has undergone a deformation which makes it incapable of any precise application whatever.

But let us allow Anatole France to speak to this point for himself, as he has undertaken to do in a passage of whose literary brilliancy my translation, I am afraid, will convey but a very imperfect idea:

Æsthetics rest on nothing really substantial; it is but a castle in the air. There has been an attempt made to support it upon ethics. But there is no such thing as an ethics—or a sociology, or yet a biology. The sciences have never been completed save in the head of M. Auguste Comte, whose work was only prophecy. When biology is finally constituted, that is to say in several million years, it may be possible to construct a sociology. That will be an affair of centuries; and then and then only will it be feasible to rear upon solid foundations a science of æsthetics. But by that time our planet will be very old and nearing its term. The sun, whose spots disquiet us already and not without reason, will turn upon the earth a dusky, sooty face, half covered with opaque slag; and the sparse survivors of humanity, fled to the bottoms of the mines, will be less concerned to discuss the essence of the beautiful than to burn their last bits of coal among the shadows before they are overwhelmed in eternal ice.

This is just and admirable—mainly because it is free from that curious intellectual confusion which invests all attempts at "scientific criticism" so called. One may read it without that painful sense of befuddlement which is the most striking effect even of Brunetière's later writing, where the reader, who has been invited to a discussion of literature, as he supposes, finds himself set down before some lukewarm *réchauffé* of evolution, so loose and vague as to bear no recognisable relation even to anything whatever properly scientific. And yet, sensitively as M. France has felt this confusion, he has omitted to exhibit the principle on which the distinction rests. The case as between literature and science is precisely like that between consciousness and physiology. Physiology may supply the physical parallel of consciousness and in this sense may be said to explain it scientifically; while all the time the latter is so irreducible in terms of the former that if we were forced to rely upon such terms for our knowledge of it, the human spirit would be, not merely unintelligible, but actually inconceivable. We ourselves alone know what is passing under our own thatch, and the disposition of that thatch gives no clue to the domestic passions it covers. And so, just as the essential element of life eludes physiological notation, so naturally does the spirit of literature, which is the record, and the sufficient record, of that life, elude and will ever elude the analysis of science.

SAINTE-BEUVE

THE main aim of Sainte-Beuve's criticism is neither judgment nor explanation in the ordinary sense. On the one hand he pretends neither to praise nor to blame; nor on the other hand does he seek to account for the phenomena with which he deals. He simply accepts and at most attempts to *préciser* them. Properly, therefore, his criticism is no more "scientific" than it is dogmatic. For him, as for Renan, truth is something elusive, fluctuating, multiform, indefinable. He has no love for the indeterminate or equivocal, for twilight or eclipse; but he despairs with a few inflexible formulæ to express "the divine and changing faces of incomprehensible Truth." He prefers with undulatory descriptive phrases to reproduce the particular aspect immediately under his notice. Within these limits his ambition is to comprehend. And when he has analysed his subject, first on this side and then on that, in hopes to circumvent the truth, if he cannot define it, then he considers that his task has been accomplished. Like Renan, then, by virtue of his conception of knowledge as well as by the nature of his subject, he is an "artist";

for his material he is obliged to rely upon the
justness of his eye, for his execution upon the
cunning of his hand.   He does not photograph,
he uses neither compass nor rule; he sketches,
and he sketches free-hand.   But if he has all of
Renan's coyness, he has little or nothing of the
latter's foppery.   Naturally liable alike to the
vices of their own method, to the abuse of doubt
and the moral indifference of curiosity, it is
just here, significantly enough, that they begin
to part company.

The weakness of curiosity as a critical incen-
tive is that even at its best and at its farthest
remove from inquisitiveness it is still a desire to know solely for the sake of knowing—a
mere appetite, *libido sciendi*, not a taste.   The
continual casting about among indifferent
opinions gradually weakens the disposition and
power to attach oneself to any opinion at all,
and ends finally in a kind of Pyrrhonism or universal scepticism.   It may be doubted, indeed,
whether any one ever formed a genuine conviction through ignorance; that is, by sheer
lack of acquaintance with other than the one
idea.   But on the other hand it is certain that
such a conviction is not to be formed by coquetting with every passing fancy.   There must be
the desire, the will to believe—the wish to em-
brace one part or another and the resolution to
abide by that decision, whatever disadvantages

it involves, including the rejection of all other alternatives. Ideally, of course, such a choice rests upon principles. But inasmuch as curiosity, and in particular a curiosity naturally sceptical like that of Sainte-Beuve and Renan, is disinclined to admit any fixed principles whatever, such a critic finally comes to have no other motive of choice to turn his belief, if he believes at all, than that of personal preference or liking. Hence the general absorption of a curious and sceptical age in things for their own sake, in the cultivation of science and knowledge and art solely on their own account. Hence too the sceptic's engrossing interest in self, as in Montaigne's case, and his constant tendency to erect that self into an ideal—to make it his god, as in Renan's case, the study of whose later writings shows clearly enough the workings of this melancholy process of hallucination and self-deception. If the sceptic happens to have a noble nature or a strong character, this insistence upon self is not so bad. In that instance his action and his thought have in reality their roots in a fairly consistent principle—in the man himself. But with a man like Renan of a feeble *morale*, which seemed to go on deteriorating from day to day, the effects are fatal.

To the superficial reader it may seem at first blush no better than a quibble to insist that Sainte-Beuve has stopped short of this danger

line while Renan has overpassed it. But that
the former has preserved a kind of personal
integrity which the latter has lost, is, I think,
clear on a little consideration. Both seem at
times dangerously near the fatal conviction
that truth is finally to be won, like a reluctant
mistress, by coquetting with a number of false
divinities to begin with. But every one must
feel in the end a difference in the temper of the
two men. Sainte-Beuve speaks—in some letter,
I believe—of the tedium of a life without God,
taking to himself the old theological curse pro-
nounced upon the infidel—"When Christianity
retires from the soul, they say, it leaves a void
and a desert such as were never known before."
And yet the curious thing is that these men
assume to have rescued a religion of some kind
from the general shipwreck of faith which they
are always bewailing. Either that, or else they
are guilty of using words in a purely conventional and traditional sense without attaching
any definite meaning to them. There is no
name more frequently on Renan's lips, even
in his *Future of Science,* than God or divinity
or its equivalent; while Sainte-Beuve reproves
the eighteenth century for nothing more sternly
and more self-righteously than for its irreverence.
And yet the latter, though he seems, like Renan,
to have made his own religion to consist in a
reverence of the ideal, appears, instead of iden-

tifying it with himself, to have set it above his head. His religion, then, as far as it is permissible to speak of his having a religion, results from the belief that there is something somewhere of more consequence than himself, and as such requires a certain amount of faith.

With sentiments of relative justice and even humanity, Frederic [the Great] was absolutely lacking, like all his age, in a sense of the ideal—he believed in nothing better than himself. The peoples who were confided to his charge he guided and cared for energetically; in this duty he set his honour and his dignity; but he did not establish it on high. This, indeed, is the cardinal vice of Frederic's wisdom—his irreverence, his irreligion.

To be sure, this is all pretty vague and unsatisfactory even as a matter of abstract speculation. The real source of Sainte-Beuve's strength lies rather in the fact that he kept his moral ideas fairly clear of confusion. It is the fashion just now to make much of his lapses; and it is well, I suppose, in the interest of our own moral ideas that there should exist no confusion as to the significance of his conduct. But what is too often forgotten is the circumstance that his lapses, while damnable in themselves, were in a manner foreign to his real being. I would not seem to diminish his responsibility or to apologise for him. A critic does his subject small service in seeking to excuse his obvious faults. But I would call attention to the fact that these faults were impertinent and irrelevant to the real Sainte-Beuve. They did not corrode the metal and infect the tissue as Renan's did, though the latter's seem in themselves much less serious. He could still distinguish between right and wrong, between good and evil, *deteriora sequens;* he had still preserved his moral integrity—and hence the superior firmness of his tone as compared with the kind of *mollesse* or flabbiness which comes to be characteristic of Renan's. He would have been incapable of fleering at his own virtues, like the latter, or congratulating himself, at the end of his life, on having been an agreeable and compliant liar.

On the other hand, successful as Sainte-Beuve was on the whole in escaping this one source of confusion, he has not always succeeded in avoiding a certain kind of literary or critical ambiguousness. For all his fondness for the *genre tranché* he is not always himself quite clear and unclouded. There are some matters where he admits a degree of vagueness. For one thing it is with him that what may be called the secularisation of letters really begins. In his own person he represents the dubious transitional term from literature to "journalism," not only in his articles where the influence of the newspaper is unmistakable, but also in his willingness to consider all sorts of writings on equal terms. In his eyes an author and his book are to all intents and purposes identical. Writing is only one among the many activities of life, only one of a thousand means of expression, though it has the advantage for his purpose of being more permanent and revelatory than another. It is from this point of view that genius and heroism look to him much the same thing—or at least merely different aspects of the same thing. "There is a moment," he says, "when invention or creation of every sort, what is called genius, heroism, begins." In other words genius is simply one manifestation of energy as heroism is another. Whether a man acts or writes, it is all the same. The real matter of interest, after all, is not the book—would he have gone so far with the act also?—but the man behind it. It makes very little difference whether the book is a by-product, a mere opuscule, a memoir, a collection of letters, a monograph, a political pamphlet; it is uniformly interesting if only the personality behind it is interesting, as an hieroglyph of character. Such is his position; and it coincides pretty accurately with that sense of the modern public to which a book is a book for a' that and everything that is written or printed is indiscriminately literature. And while he has in this way contributed largely to the information of the public, he has also done as much to befuddle the popular notion of letters and to assist that confusion of literature with life which we have only too good reason to lament at present. "If men wrote as well as they talk or if some one were to write down for them what they say in the decisive moments of their life, there would be a quantity of writers who would be only the more memorable for not having been bred to the business." This is exactly the idea that the magazines have been clever enough to perceive and enterprising enough to carry out—with disastrous effect to letters.

But unfortunately the confusion, which is bad enough in reducing the literary and the documentary to a common level, does not end there. As a matter of fact Sainte-Beuve finally develops, if anything, a kind of prejudice against literature as such. Not infrequently he will discriminate against what is written with care and intention in favour of the inadvertent and casual, even when the latter is clearly inferior, provided only there is some kind of personal disclosure about it. Of Malherbe's letters he remarks:

The best are those which he wrote as he talked, at the corner of the fire. Many of them are incorrect, many are flat, though at the same time they are curious for the facts and the sensible observations which are mingled with them. Such are his letters to Peiresc, which answer very ill to the idea that they were written by a poet, but which are those of a man of sense transmitting, to another man of sense, reports and gazettes of the events of which he is a witness.

Ingenuously one would suppose an author
interesting mainly for his literary work. But
Sainte-Beuve is more professional, and, what is
worse, allows his professional preoccupations to
slip into his writing. As a critic with an article
or two a week on his hands, he is always on the
piste of a subject; and it happens often enough
that the chief interest of his subject even in his
own eyes consists in the circumstance that he has
a use for it. To the critical imagination, too,
confronted with its engagements, this particular
sort of subject, which is neither a matter of life
nor yet of literature exclusively, but which stands
as an intermediate term between the two, has
no doubt a peculiar fascination. It still belongs
to the library and the study rather than to the
street or market-place; it is mastered by reading
rather than observation; and it has already been
submitted to a partial organisation or interpretation, which is just sufficient to stimulate the
critic to his own manner of composition without
obliging him to draw his materials directly from
the inchoate welter of immediate experience.
It is still the book, the letter, in which he finds
his inspiration. But, whatever its excuse or
explanation, this frequent reserve or reticence
which Sainte-Beuve comes to evince for a work
of art, as compared with his enthusiasm and ex-
pansiveness in the presence of a document, can
not fail to irritate and even disconcert the general

reader. To contrast his grudgingness towards Lamartine's recollections with his freehandedness towards Frederic the Great's correspondence, you would suppose the former a very inferior performance indeed. And in fact this habit of meeting *paperasse* with open arms and a cheerful alacrity to make the best of it regardlessly, gives his criticism on the whole a strange look of distortion, like a Chinese picture with its impossible perspectives and crazy proportions. It is in some such fashion as this that Sainte-Beuve, who is all for the *genre tranché*, inoculates the body of letters with his own little bacillus of deformation, and, while confusing journalism and literature, creates at the same time a kind of nondescript criticism, which is neither literary nor historical, but a cross between the two.

As a matter of fact, whatever I may seem to have implied for the moment, his aim was not restricted to characterisation and analysis in the ordinary or narrower sense. In addition he seems to have had before his eyes some flickering notion of a kind of systematic description and classification of characters, a natural history of the human spirit—a scheme which recalls Balzac's extravagant pretensions in the *Comédie Humaine*. The philosophic basis of the idea may be gathered from his own words:

The actual number of *natural* human families is not so very great. When one has looked about him a little

—

with this thought in mind and has got together a sufficient quantity of observations, he recognises how easily all varieties of human intelligence and organisation are referable to certain types, to certain leading heads or principals. Such and such a notable contemporary, whom you have seen and comprehended, explains and recalls a whole series of the dead, from the moment that you recognise his essential resemblance with them and that your eye is caught by certain family characteristics. It is just as with plants in botany or animals in zoölogy. There is a moral natural history, the method, hardly sketched as yet, of natural families of human beings. On observation an individual is quickly referred to the species which has been seen only from a distance, and explains it.

However suggestive as an *aperçu*, this is not very lucid as a scientific prospectus. But the age was given to just such vague and grandiose speculations in commerce and business as well as in philosophy and literature. And it is curious to see Sainte-Beuve too, for all his natural caution, enveloping himself majestically with the folds of an equally pretentious and nebulous conception.

Nevertheless it is doubtful whether such pretensions had very much effect upon the character of his criticism, which is by no means so far removed from the traditional desires and ambitions of its kind as might at first appear. Whatever its profession, that criticism does, in reality, involve an explanation and a judgment, though it may seldom or never pronounce one.

For inasmuch as the critic undertook to attribute the book to its author, he did in so far account for it; while by the very circumstance of setting out its intimate character, as a reflection of the author's, he was unable to avoid such a grouping and accentuation of detail as amounted to a sentence of approval or the contrary. With regard to the justice of these implicit judgments the general reader and the casual critic are frequently obliged to rely upon the testimony of his compatriots and other second-hand evidence, on account of the character of many of his subjects, which are comparatively seldom of first-rate importance by any means, to say nothing of the nature of his interests. To a person who is concerned principally with literature in the more exclusive sense, he is bound, I suppose, to seem disappointing—at least to begin with. He is, if anything, over-cautious, particularly in enunciating general principles or in eliciting them from his subject. He depends too much upon names and dates and little registers—to be sure, if he had not filled his hold with the like ballast, he could hardly have made his weekly trips with such commendable steadiness and punctuality. Nor does he always supply the want of literary interest by a moral or human one; it happens but too frequently that at best he is only physiological. In many cases he is safe except from the special and erudite scholar.

And yet there are instances where it is possible
for us, who have no such gloomy and impressive
pretensions, to catch him in error, either with
regard to matters of taste or of general view and
opinion. And so it is that a little suspicion of
his infallibility will slip into our estimate, confirmed by several considerations patent to every
one, French or foreigner, learned or simple.

In his criticism of his contemporaries, for instance, there is something very like an animus
which results in distorting to some extent his
view of the literature of his own time, and so
numerous and delicate are the attachments of
the critical judgment, in warping his view of the
literature of all time. In particular he seems
to envy them their hold upon the youth and
perhaps a little their success with the ladies,
and to take a malicious pleasure in exposing
the futility of this flattering *clientèle*. In this
sort his articles on Lamartine's *Confidences* and
Raphaël seem in some way to be inadvertently
confidential and revelatory of that little sedi-
ment of disappointment and chargin which
have settled in the heart of the author *manqué*
of *Joseph Delorme* and *Volupté*. In the latter
of these two articles *Raphaël* and Lamartine
along with it are despatched in the following
workmanlike and satisfactory manner—a thoroughly good example of Sainte-Beuve's critical
execution:

Works of this sort, which have been adopted by the generation wherein they were born, which can be read in couples, and with which, so to speak, one makes love, are extremely nice to analyse. It seems as though the critic, in undertaking to point out what shocks and astonishes him, were meddling with private and treasured sentiments and were playing the part of a wet blanket. M. Lamartine knows it; and some time since I was assured that he had been heard to say: "What's the difference! Let them say all they please; the ladies and the young men are always on my side." Charming and desirable auditory no doubt, but by no means definitive. The youth themselves cease to be young; and some day when they happen to think of rereading you, they are amazed. Then other generations quickly succeed, who do not allow themselves to be captivated by the same faults, who bear others a grudge for doing so, and who wish especially to have the mode and fashion of their sentiments renewed. Then the faded volume is judged solely for the weight of its gifts and merits. It is of this stern to-morrow that every serious artist ought to think. To be sure, M. Lamartine in the intoxication of his success may believe that such a to-morrow will never dawn for him. It is now thirty years since he published his meditations and fired the choicest youth of the day. Thirty years later there he is again with this same Elvire transformed into Julie, in hopes perhaps of carrying away the youth once more. But he has greatly deceived himself, we are sure, if he fancies that he has done so; the seduction is no longer the same, or without alloy. It is not yet exhausted, however; and in the destiny of the poet who has charmed both fathers and sons with this same theme of love, there is something that recalls the destiny of Ninon. But be that as it may, sooner or later breaks the fatal morrow.

This is just as well as shrewd. But surely the critic was not inconsolable that he was able to be shrewd as well as just. And it is not impossible that it is his envy which has helped him to find his way to his author's weakness. His *Préface pour les Maximes de la Rochefoucauld* looks superficially as though it had been written expressly for the purpose of airing a few of these spites, and recalls, distressingly enough, an entry of the Goncourts' journal:

If one only knew what moves Sainte-Beuve to make a book! We found him to-day fired by a project for a publication on Mme. de Staël and her group . . . and that not by interest or curiosity in Mme. de Staël's memory or even by the seduction of unpublished manuscripts, but simply for the sake of being disagreeable to the Broglies, whom he detests.

Between these two natures there was instinctive antipathy enough to invalidate the Goncourts' general estimate of Sainte-Beuve; and yet in this respect there is enough truth in their remark to give it a terrible pertinency:

Allons, to the last, even on the edge of his grave Sainte-Beuve will be the same Sainte-Beuve he has always been—a man whose criticism is influenced by infinitely slight and petty considerations, by personal questions, by the pressure of the domestic opinions about him.

And, while the remark is neither exact nor measured, still it is hardly possible to under-

stand Sainte-Beuve's attitude without reckoning
in this sense of disappointment and mortification, this sourness against those who succeeded
where he had failed. The thoroughness of
his reaction against the literary tendencies of
his day, against lyricism, against romanticism,
against whatever he had sought and failed to
make his own, bears witness to a degree of disillusion which is seldom reached save through a
sick stomach. One who reads him even care-
lessly is constantly aware of some force re-
pelling him from the present to its contrary
pole and intensifying the vehemence of his
revolt. "*À tel chapitre vanté d'un roman
moderne, on opposerait un recit de Xavier de
Maistre,*" he recommends in his article *des Lectures publiques.* And the *procédé* is so habitually
his own that it comes to resemble a *parti pris*, a
preconceived idea of literary excellence, which,
whatever its motive, does, as a matter of fact,
result in a disturbance of his critical equilibrium.

It is necessary, however, to distinguish.
That Sainte-Beuve had sufficient cause for personally disliking Balzac, is conceivable. It is
not pleasant to have a boisterous rival threaten
to make over your failures and produce a *Lys
dans la Vallée* for a *Volupté;* hardly more so to
have him compare your style to a drizzle drench-
ing the reader with melancholy to the marrow
of his bones. And yet for all this provocation

Sainte-Beuve's estimate of Balzac is undoubtedly nearer the mark than Brunetière's immoderate praise. In like manner the Goncourts get a good deal more attention from us than they deserve or than they ever succceeded in getting from Sainte-Beuve, however mixed his motives for slighting them. And just so in a good many other cases it will be found in the end, I believe, that he is more often right than current criticism likes to acknowledge. It is not, then, his mistakes with reference to this author or that, or altogether the mixture of his motives—although a mixture of motives does introduce a very undesirable confusion into criticism; it is rather the flaw in that universal sympathy, that general and unfailing receptivity and responsiveness to which he pretended and which his criticism demanded for its highest success— that break of electric connection which has rendered defective in some measure the intimacy of his communion with every variety of the human spirit.

And what is so melancholy about the whole matter, after all, is the fact that a man like Sainte-Beuve should have allowed his mind to be troubled—for troubled to some extent it was —by a petty jealousy of his contemporaries when he was himself creating single-handed a criticism which unlike most criticism is a literary *genre* of itself and by which his name will be always illustrated. What that *genre* actually was, when disentangled from the vague and ambitious theories with which he occasionally sought to mystify and aggrandise it, may be described best in his own words:

In the range of criticism and literary history there is no reading, it seems to me, more entertaining, enjoyable, and at the same time instructive in every way, than good lives of great men; not shallow and dry biographies, scanty yet pretentious notices, where the writer thinks only of shining, and where every paragraph is pointed with an epigram. I mean broad, copious, even diffuse histories of a man and his works; biographies that enter into an author, produce him under all his different aspects, make him live, speak, move as he must have done in life; follow him into his home, into his domestic manners and customs, as far as possible; connect him on all sides with this earth, with real existence, with those every-day habits on which great men depend no less than the rest of us; in short, the actual foundation on which they stand, from which they rise to greater heights at times, and to which they fall back continually.

This is Sainte-Beuve's ideal of criticism; it is what he tried to do himself and what on the whole he succeeded in doing. That it is by no means a *genre tranché*, is evident. It is crossed with other species of one sort and another; it is confused with vague and grandiose pretensions; it is clouded with personal passion and prejudice. And what is more important, it proposes to itself an end impossible of complete attainment; for such a criticism as this is nothing less than a criticism of human nature as a whole. Other critics, in restricting themselves to some particular point of view or to some particular topic, in considering the author merely as a literary creature or in looking at nothing but poetry or history, have reduced their liability considerably and have been able at the same time to take advantage of the methodical limitations of their subject or point of view. Consider how Matthew Arnold helps himself by leaving out his contemporaries and taking account only of first-rate talent, which has already acquired a more or less recognised standing. And yet even with this assistance he goes astray occasionally—patently so in admitting Maurice de Guérin into a company of which he is by no means the equal. But Sainte-Beuve's is no special criticism in any sense; on the contrary it begins by renouncing all such adscititious aids and advantages. It is the criticism neither of this one subject nor of that; it is not even the criticism of genius exclusively. It is the criticism of human nature as a whole; and in appropriating the universally human it deliberately deprives itself of any particular restraint or protection—it has to depend solely upon the elasticity of the critic's spirit and the flexibility of his style. In so doing it amounts to a denial of all method, of formulæ and equations and definitions, of every aid and

accessory of the unassisted intelligence. It is
mainly an affair of shading, and consists in the
ability to detect and reproduce the most delicate
gradations, the most elusive interplay of light
and shadow; while, as it creeps on from subject
to subject and from period to period, it implies
nothing less for its perfection than absolute
universality of mind and sympathy on the part
of its wielder. And this is its weakness exactly.
Sainte-Beuve's genius was by no means universal; it is much more sensitive on some sides than
on others. Not only are his subjects not always
of first-rate importance, as indeed there is no
reason that they should be; not only are his
criticisms of his contemporaries subject to
personal prejudice and bias, which seriously
derange his general scale of values—he has also
his blind sides and callous spots, which betray
themselves unmistakably every now and then
by some uncertainty of touch or dissonance of
tone.

A man who undertakes a colossal task like
this of Sainte-Beuve's must soon come to feel
and to act as though he had a part to play. He
can hardly afford, nor can he bear, to acknowledge himself ignorant or incapable at any point;
and yet, short of omniscience, it is impossible
that he should possess all the knowledge, all the
faculty to which he has tacitly laid claim. The
wonder is that Sainte-Beuve should have

tripped so seldom, not that he should have tripped at all or that he should break down in those rôles which are naturally the hardest to sustain—those involving sensibility and tact, in particular the analysis of the intricacies of the feminine heart. Upon violations of delicacy and taste Sainte-Beuve bears very heavily in the case of others—probably because an air of authority in such matters is supposed to confer immediate distinction. For the dubious and the equivocal he seems to have had an astonishingly keen scent and to have delighted in turning them up for the mortification of their author, when another would ordinarily pass by, at least without unearthing them. As soon as the sharp-nosed critic has once stirred the air, it is impossible, no doubt, to ignore his disclosures. But there is a certain order of ideas which the critic must have in mind in order to remark them at all—an order of ideas "*que c'est presque une indélicatesse à la critique elle-même de venir relever.*" Upon Lamartine in particular he is, as usual, very severe for the manner in which he speaks of his mother.

And, *par example*, not to go outside of the *Confidences*, with regard to matters of taste and sentiment, what does M. de Lamartine do when he speaks of his mother? He is not satisfied to sketch her portrait, he describes her. To describe with such evident unction a person who is so nearly related to us, and whom we stand so many chances of resembling, declares in

itself a want of tact for a subject so delicate. And
in what terms does he describe her!

After such a lesson in propriety and *savoir
vivre* it is not a little amusing to read his own
article on the Duchesse d'Angoulême, upon
whose simplicity of "*apparat*" he remarks with
a kind of naïve and snobbish wonder that a
grande dame should be a woman after all.

But it is only when he allows his vanity as a
feminist to get the better of him that Sainte-
Beuve is at his worst. To the ladies he is
always infinitely condescending; but, what is
still worse, he is often infinitely knowing.
Because he has had the run of the town for years,
he feels himself quite at ease in Zion. In his
manner toward the great ladies at such times
he is singularly like Balzac. It is edifying to
compare his gallantry to Mmes. de la Fayette
and Longueville, for instance, with his table
talk of the sex in general, as reported by the
unconscionable Goncourt under the date of
June 22, 1863. But alas! the passage is quite
unquotable. Nor is his touch for religious
subjects much more sure. What a man of intelligence, trusting infatuately in the strength
of his own understanding, can do in this kind,
he has done in *Port-Royal*. With a number, by
no means small, of happy exceptions it is as
a whole a stupendous monument of factitious
devoutness and of questionable taste that has

its roots in a lack of profound conviction. As in all these cases, it is not so much the mere forcing of a note or the surcharging of a trait which is so lamentable, as the kind of insincerity which results from this Napoleonic greed of universal empire, this constant pretension to unlimited comprehension—an insincerity which in a smaller man breathing no other air than this might have led to downright charlatanism or hypocrisy. It may be only fancy—no doubt it is so—but nevertheless I seem to detect even in Sainte-Beuve the critic something of that double and ambiguous character which Goncourt saw in Sainte-Beuve the man:

To-day Eudore Soulié said with perfect justice that there are two Sainte-Beuves: the Sainte-Beuve of the upper story, of the workroom and the study, the man of thought and reflection; and quite another Sainte-Beuve, the Sainte-Beuve of the ground floor, the man of the dining-room and the family circle, surrounded by the *manchote*, his mistress, by Marie, his cook, and by his two maids. In this company Sainte-Beuve becomes a *petit bourgeois*, insensible to all the grandeur of his life above stairs, a sort of shop-keeper at a free and easy, his mind bounded by the women's imbecile tittle-tattle, asininities, and twaddle.

It would be imprudent, no doubt, to lay very much emphasis on any opinion of Sainte-Beuve reported by Goncourt. And yet does not such a distinction occasionally obtrude itself, as between a Sainte-Beuve of "the ground floor," touchy, agitated by jealousy and petty passion, envenoming his criticism with his personal spites and animosities, inflated with vanity and presumption, abusing the prophetic office for the denunciation of his private enemies, and the Sainte-Beuve of the judgment seat, dispensing justice, high, even-handed, inexorable, inspired by the spirit of a great tradition, anticipating the fatal sentence of posterity, a Sainte-Beuve not unworthy of a place with Boileau, the particular object of his admiration, and one not inferior, in that Pantheon *"de tous les nobles humains, de tous ceux qui ont accru pour une part notable et durable la somme des jouissances et des titres de l'esprit,"* which he has himself so eloquently described? For after all in comparison with the scope of his work these are but small flaws and imperfections, mere blots and blemishes, inherent almost in the character of the undertaking, which the extent of that undertaking reduces to insignificant proportions.

For this reason there is one side of his criticism where he is at a more serious, because a less inevitable, disadvantage. For the kind of thing that he undertook, for the portraiture of man, he lacked one essential faculty. His analysis is of the keenest; he can take down and demonstrate the machine, no matter how complicated, with marvellous deftness, accuracy, and clearness. He can dismember and articulate the literary skeleton bone by bone. But he is wanting in that magical touch which like a play of light and shadow seems for an instant to inspire the motionless features of the subject with a flicker of life. In all his criticism there is, as far as I can remember, no such vivid evocation as that whereby Maupassant, in general a very indifferent critic indeed, conjures up the melancholy figure of Flaubert standing in his window and staring vacantly at the passers up and down the Seine.

Certainly in some sorts of criticism such faculty would never be missed. Indeed, it is the property of the dramatist or the novelist rather than that of the critic. "Crusoe recoiling from the footprint, Achilles shouting over against the Trojans, Ulysses bending the great bow, Christian running with his fingers in his ears"—these, says Stevenson, are "the epoch-making scenes, which put the last mark of truth upon a story and fill up, at one blow, our capacity for sympathetic pleasure." And it is probably Sainte-Beuve's deficiency in this sort of power which underlay his failure as a novelist, if not as a poet. But at the same time it is just the distinction of his criticism that it is not exclusively a criticism of general ideas and principles. As a matter of fact it has been reproached for dealing in such matters too little. And the case is the more curious because some of the very best of his essays are of this sort—"What is a Classic?" "Mme. de Caylus and What is Known as Urbanity," "Literary Tradition," and so on. But from this order of considerations he was constantly diverted by "journalism" and his desire for a kind of official popularity. And it was obviously impossible to produce a criticism of principles in weekly instalments; nor would such a criticism have suited his public. Hence the *petits faits divers*, the assorted news-items, the historical and biographical miscellany, which form the bulk of his cargo. And he was drawn in the same direction, very much as Molière seems to have been drawn toward tragedy, by the natural gravitation of his tastes. If he could not be a novelist, he would come as near to being one as he could; he would build on a foundation of fact the same kind of edifice as Balzac was even then rearing amid the clouds and vapours of the imagination. As a result his criticism has become, in the literal terms of Matthew Arnold's definition, though in a more precise sense than can ever be true of poetry, a "criticism of life." At the same time that it is on the one part a cross between journalism and scholarship, in the old acceptation of the latter word, it is also, on the other part, a cross between the more analytic and the more creative forms of literature. And it should in its kind combine the dissections of criticism with the plasticity of the novel. It ought at one moment to be ready to disentangle the idea from the clutter of accompanying circumstance and hold it up to contemplation as something universal and inalterable; and it ought again to be able to fuse idea and circumstance into a perfect, if momentary, illusion of reality. And in as far as it is powerless to fulfil either of these requirements, it falls short, to just that extent, of its proper perfection and the complete realisation of its own ideal.

But, after all, such considerations, though they may be true as far as they go, are in a larger sense more or less irrelevant. It is not on method that Sainte-Beuve's case finally rests, as Taine's does, but on his sense for life, no matter what *lacunæ* may occur in his knowledge, no matter what presentation or expression he may elect to give it. Of method, indeed, that sense is the direct contradiction. In Pascal's *Pensées* there is an interesting passage where, seeking apparently to find his own way into literature, he attempts to distinguish this sense for life, "the spirit of finesse," as he calls it, from the sense for method, as represented by "the spirit of geometry":

With respect to the spirit of finesse, he says, the principles are in common use and under every one's eyes. And he continues after a little: But they are hardly to be seen; they are felt rather than seen. And it is infinitely difficult to show them to him who does not

feel them for himself. They are so fine and so numerous that it requires a very clear and delicate perception
to appreciate them at all and to judge justly and accurately in accordance with this sentiment, since they
can not be demonstrated systematically as in geometry.
. . . The point must be caught instantaneously, at
a single glance, not by a process of reasoning. . . . Not
that the mind does not reason at all in such cases, but
it does so tacitly, naturally, and artlessly, for the expression of the matter is too much for most men and
the feel of it belongs only to a few.

There could be no better characterisation;
such is the spirit of Sainte-Beuve's criticism.
He had his *procédés*, no doubt. He was much
concerned to convert his subjects into articles
for his journal; and I have mentioned certain
distortions which resulted from the process.
But it is necessary to grant him his vehicle and
its inconveniences—no one has ever escaped
them, not even Pascal himself. But for what is
contained therein—for observation and reflection, for example and object-lesson, for maxim
and aphorism, above all for sound moral ideas
—these articles, *leçons*, or what not, occasional,
journalistic, and otherwise, offer to the student
of human nature one of the richest of intellectual
treasures. For this sense of life, this "spirit
of finesse," which animates Sainte-Beuve's work
and which gives it a permanent and universal
significance and constitutes it literature—what
is this spirit after all but wisdom?

EMERSON AND THE MODERN REPORTS

BY general consent Emerson's fundamental weakness as an author resides in his form. There are few writers of his eminence whose instrument is of so small a compass. He is a poet, a critic, and a moralist; but his style is incapable of passion, *suite*, and humour. When he is amusing, he is so unconsciously and by reason of his lack of humour, rather than of his possession of it.

A great man is coming to eat at my house. 1 do not wish to please him. I wish that he should wish to please me. I will stand here for humanity, and though I would make it kind, I would make it true.

In the mouth of the lean, high-cheeked, provincial Yankee, who ate his pie for breakfast, such a remark may seem funny enough. But Emerson never intended it to be funny. Indeed, his seriousness, his preternatural unruffled gravity, is one of his most marked characteristics, as it is that of the little group of *illuminati* to which he belonged; while as for wit, if he seem not entirely deficient in that good gift also, the exception is due in part to the paradoxical and antithetical turn of his mind, which gives an unexpected and striking twist to the most ordinary sentiments.

That he felt keenly, I suppose we can hardly doubt. And yet even in his best poetry he is seldom or never fired with the passionate intensity of the great poets. The verse of his that I remember best—indeed, it is almost the only verse of his that I remember at all—is this:

> So nigh is grandeur to our dust,
> So near is God to man,
> When duty whispers, Lo, thou must,
> The youth replies, I can.

This is not bad, whatever the modern criticaster may say of it. But it lacks the afflatus. It has feeling, but no passion, either of the heart or the imagination. For among other things passion implies a fluency of expression, a willingness or ability to let oneself go under the accumulated pressure of emotion, which is thoroughly inconsistent with Emerson's rigidity both in prose and verse. For a great writer his phrase is always singularly cramped and scanty, and particularly lacking in that free discursive development which makes one of the characteristic excellences of prose, just as it is in the fervent concentration characteristic of poetry. While Newman has an amplitude of expression, a flow of explanation and illustration which seems inexhaustible, Emerson can hardly turn more than two or three sentences without a complete change of topic. It seems as though truth flashed upon him, like a clear star upon a world without an atmosphere, in a single point of great brilliancy but without dimension. There is no diffusion about his thought; it refuses to flow or dilate. It congeals into crystalline particles like tiny icicles. His best things are mostly sentences or phrases dropped by the way like seeds, which may take root and flower in the new soil but which always find their growth outside the author's mind.

Society is everywhere in conspiracy against the manhood of every one of its members.
A foolish consistency is the hobgoblin of little minds.
An institution is the lengthened shadow of one man.
To be great is to be misunderstood.
Prayer is the contemplation of the facts of life from the highest point of view.

In this way his essays have become, as it were, a collection of centres of force or influence, so that it would be a mistake to expect of one of them the continuous evolution of a single theme, or to look below the surface for a thoroughly definite plan or structure. Properly they are not compositions at all—rather accumulations of *pensées* or maxims which he has believed to be worth saving, thrown together around some common motive—an aggregation, not an organism, loosely held together by a single title like a string around a parcel. He himself has suggested as much in his *Self-Reliance*.

In this pleasing contrite wood life which God allows me, let me record day by day my honest thought without prospect or retrospect, and, I can not doubt, it will be found symmetrical, though I mean it not and see it not.

In short Emerson's is naturally a fragmentary style, a *brachylogia*, like that of the German romanticists, like Friedrich Schlegel's and in particular like Novalis's, who had apparently any number of ideas in his head, which never grew and ramified, who saw things bright and clear and steady, but only at a single angle, without parallax or diffraction, but who, less fortunate or more feeble than Emerson, was never able to sweep his thoughts together with even so much semblance of consecutiveness as the latter succeeded in attaining. Or rather, if you please, we may look upon Emerson as an aphorist or epigrammatist, for whom thought bunches up into little tight bundles, who finds, so to speak, the point of an idea in the knot that he ties it into, and who would feel a fatal flatness in spinning out the thread of his thought and weaving it into a broad extended web of ordinary pattern.

It is on account of this disposition to see things singly, if brilliantly, like so many stars

in a clear sky, to look at a single aspect of a
matter to the exclusion of all others, that Emerson incurs his most curious and amusing fault—
the jumbling together of a number of particu-
lars whose conjunction is only ridiculous or
disconcerting. "Consider whether you have
satisfied your relations to father, mother, cousin,
neighbour, town, cat, and dog; whether any
of these can upbraid you." At first thought
the sentence sounds like Mark Twain; a moment's reflection reveals its identity with Walt
Whitman. Whether Walt Whitman consciously
formed himself on Emerson or not, this is at
all events as much of his master as he succeeded
in appropriating; and as far as it goes it is very
like.

"We do not yet see that virtue is Height,
and that a man or a company of men, plastic
and permeable to principles, by the law of
nature, must overpower and ride all cities,
nations, kings, rich men, poets, who are not."
Undoubtedly Emerson wrote the passage; but all
the same it is Whitman to a T. The "plastic
and permeable to principles" has his very twang,
to say nothing of the repetition, "a man or a
company of men," and the final enumeration,
"all cities, nations, kings, rich men, poets."
Compare it, for example, with Whitman's self:

Perhaps the best of songs heard, or of any and all
true love, or life's finest episodes, or sailors', soldiers',

trying scenes on land or sea, is the résumé of them, or
any of them, long afterwards, looking at the actualities
away back past, with their practical excitations gone.

We need, perhaps, to be reminded that this
sort of thing is not a joke—hardly that it is not
literature any more than a catalogue or an
inventory; and that, in as far as it is representative of Emerson at all, it is so only as a man's
bad habits may be representative in showing
his constitutional failings, or as a caricature
resembles the original in exaggerating his fatal
peculiarities. In such a sense the quotations
merit a place here only as they serve to explain
the hereditary weakness of Emerson's intellectual descendants—of all those who have made
themselves inheritors of his logical inconse-
quence, and more particularly as they show how
Emerson himself is to be taken. To expect of
him, much less of these heirs of his, the rigid
consistency of thought which marks a man like
Matthew Arnold or the elaborately concatenated
philosophy of a Herbert Spencer, would be to
miss the mark entirely. It is enough to pick
up by the way such suggestions as he lets drop
and at the same time to catch in a general way
the run—or perhaps I should say the drift—of
his thought as a whole.

When good is near you, when you have life in yourself, it is not by any known or accustomed way; you
shall not discern the footprints of any other; you shall

not see the face of man; you shall not hear any name;—
the way, the thought, the good shall be wholly strange
and new.

This is Emerson pretty nearly at his best.
How picturesquely and tellingly he puts again
the familiar old sensation—the vain conceit that
wisdom is born with us!

And yet however dazzling these sudden splen-
dours—and, if anything, too much has been
made of them of late to the disparagement of the
deeper Emerson—it is even more important, as
I have just implied, to catch the general drift
of his thought as a whole. For as he himself observes, while his writing is lacking in the more
rigid sort of coherence, it has still the consecutiveness of his character. However his mood
shifts, it is the same man who writes through
all. And while he may neglect to contrive a
formal transition as between his ideas, yet the
general uniformity of his character will declare
itself with respect to his work in an inclination
to make, on the whole, in a certain definite
direction. And this is no small matter. It is
just in this particular that he is so immeasur-
ably superior to his followers. For, though his
philosophy may be unmethodical and quite
without "coherent, interdependent, subordinate,
and derivative" principles, there have been few
men who were themselves so integral, so thoroughly of a piece. He may have no system,

but he has a disposition. And of this larger current or steady bearing of his thought, as distinguished from those flashes of intuition already spoken of, there is probably no better example, as there is no more timely one, than that which is furnished by his ideas on the subject started by the last quotation from *Self-Reliance*, a subject which for want of a better name I may be allowed to call the institution of truth.

Superficially the essay on self-reliance is a reckless glorification of individualism. Truth, in this conception, is to be found within—and the latter part of the essay attempts, not very successfully, to show how it came there. Originality consists in differing with your neighbours; genius, in the conviction that whatever you think, is so, and in the determination to impose it upon every one else too. He alone is independent who has shaken himself free of all institutions, organisations, societies, creeds, conventions, received opinions, and what not. Only when alone are you in good company; only when agreeing with yourself are you in the right. "The only right is after my own constitution; the only wrong is against it." On second thoughts, however, you had better not agree even with yourself; for in so doing you are likely to become a slave to self-consistency, "the hobgoblin of little minds."

As for all this rhapsodical assertion it may be

taken in either of two ways, absolutely or relatively. Taken absolutely and in the literal
sense it is obviously false. It is not even on
reasonably good terms with itself. At the
same time that it proposes originality as the
sole object of our admiration and the main end
of our being, it represents genius as a standing
menace to human liberty, as the greater light
puts out the less. "An institution is the lengthened shadow of one man"—and, he should have
added, eclipses a thousand. Nevertheless it is
instructive to notice the correspondence between
these ideas and the characteristic peculiarities
of his form, his sententiousness and inconse-
quence, and to see the manner in which the former explain the latter. If truth is personal and
a matter of inspiration, it is idle to talk about
it. Discussion, explanation, argument are alike
unavailing. Either it dawns upon the spirit
instantaneously and by a kind of divination, or
it never dawns at all. And just as it varies
from individual to individual, so too it is likely
to vary from one moment to another, for the
observer is never twice alike.

For my own part I am quite ready to admit
that truth is many-sided and has a face for
everybody—even while I sometimes suspect
that the illusion may be due to the imperfection
of our faculty, and that if we could once see it
as it is, it would appear amazingly simple and

achromatic—yet under any circumstances, even
speculatively it is preposterous to propose di-
versity as a standard. To assert that there
are as many truths as persons, is to deny the
existence of truth altogether. If everything
is true, then truth is nothing—or at all events
it is a matter of indifference. For such an
opinion there is, indeed, a good deal to be said;
but such is not Emerson's argument. He does
not contend even for the relativity of truth,
which is much the same thing under another
name, as do Renan and Sainte-Beuve. On
the contrary his notion of truth is singularly
absolute and inflexible—so absolute and inflexible, in fact, as to carry with it a moral
obligation. Of such truth, however, it is
impossible that the individual temperament
should be the criterion; it is rather a source of
error and aberration. "*Als ob der Mensch et-
was anderes aus sich selber hätte als die Dummheit
und das Ungeschick!*" Even the boy, whom
Emerson proposes as a perfect model of independent judgment, judges for the most part as
a boy and like other boys, and merely appears
singular because his judgment is not adult.
As a matter of fact there is no creature more
conventional than the school-boy. "A boy,"
says Cardinal Newman, "has opinions religious,
political, and literary; and for a boy he is very
positive in them and sure about them; but he

gets them from his school-fellows, or his masters, or his parents, as the case may be." To be
sure; as well expect independent criticism from
a drawing-room as from the playground.

And in one sense it is very fortunately so.
As far as the individual stands alone, he is
subject to error. If he ever gets on the track
at all, it is only by bringing himself into conformity with the best sense of humanity and
the permanent acquirements of human culture.
In short he has just two clues in his search for
truth—tradition and common-sense, both of
which Emerson abjures. By tradition I understand not a slavish imitation of antiquity, or a
timid attempt to perpetuate it forever, but such
a study of the past as will put the student in
possession of the accumulated experience and
wisdom of the race as it has withstood the
searching test of time, and will help him to
distinguish between the temporary, the merely
fashionable and accidental on the one hand, and
the permanent and essential on the other, and
will enable him, finally, to determine the proper
course and direction of human progress and
the proper aim and end of man and bring himself into line with them. One reason, to borrow
an illustration from literature, for the ultimate
failure of Pope and his school, is to be found in
the circumstance that they reacted against the
prevailing spirit of English poetry, the spirit

of Chaucer and Spenser and Shakespeare. They deliberately put themselves outside the stream of poetical tendency so that they neither drew from the past nor contributed to the future. And in the same way I can not help wondering sometimes whether many of our notions to-day—our arrogant materialism, our vapid and diffusive humanitarianism, and our mob democracy—are not, in reality, merely blind alleys, quite aside from the main line of march—whether they too are not clean out of the way and no thoroughfare.

Nor is tradition enough in itself. Since the times change and the old order, and the needs of yesterday are not those of to-day, it is necessary also to take into account the best sense of the age in which we are living. "The only method," declares Burke in flat contradiction to Emerson, "the only method which has ever been found effectual to preserve any man against the corruption of nature and example, is an habit of life and communication of counsels with the most virtuous and public-spirited men of the age you live in. Such a society cannot be kept without advantage or deserted without shame." And again he says, "I am aware that the age is not what we all wish." What age is? "But I am sure that the only means of checking its precipitate degeneracy is hastily to concur with whatever is best in our time."

This it is which I should like to understand by common-sense—not the mere unanimity of vulgar opinion, the bare average intelligence of humanity, but rather the consensus of enlightened opinion at any one period of history. In such a manner, then, as Burke suggests, in controlling and directing ourselves by this larger spirit which constitutes the culture of our day, we shall stand the best chance of escaping extravagance, provincialism, rusticity, and the thousand and one other failings of sectarianism and dissent, and of acquiring moderation, temperance, measure, and liberality. Indeed, it is very doubtful whether a great and permanent work of any kind was ever produced in opposition to the best agreement of the age, a work which did not absorb its ideas in large part from the surrounding atmosphere as a plant converts to higher uses the inorganic elements of its habitat. Where no such body of elevated ideas exists, as I am obliged to think is the case to-day, a great work is certainly impossible; but it is equally impossible in opposition to such a body of ideas or in neglect of it. There is Goethe's work on colour, for example, which is in its own way a very curious and ingenious performance. But it failed to fall in with the best scientific thought of the time. Goethe was impatient of the mathematical conceptions of optical science; and, as

Helmholtz remarks, he went at the matter like a poet, not like a man of science at all. To him colour was all illusion and appearance. And as a result, original in Emerson's sense though the work may be, it is altogether beside the mark; while such is the extremity into which even the dissidence of genius may be hurried, that Goethe himself professes a greater pride in the authorship of the worthless and mistaken *Farbenlehre* than in the matchless body of poetry on which his immortality depends.

On the other hand, if Emerson's essay be taken relatively as a protest against some particular vice or abuse which needs or did once need correction, then it may be necessary to modify to some extent the preceding judgment. What is required of such a protest is, not that it should hit off the exact mean, but rather that it should stress emphatically the antithesis of the vices to be reformed. To this end a great part of the criticism of every age is directed—a circumstance which makes the criticism of one age seem false and one-sided to another. In fact criticism is always the victim of its own success. As an expostulation, therefore, against intellectual servility and spiritual servitude the essay on *Self-Reliance* may have its relative justice. That the majority is no more likely to be right than is the minority, that wisdom does not reveal herself to crowds, that truth is

not published for the first time in the morning
papers, that religion is between the individual
conscience and its God—these things are undoubtedly true, and are worth repeating even
nowadays in a country which seems to think
that by multiplying together a sufficient number
of nonentities you can produce an irreproachable
substitute for genius. And in this relative
sense the essay would probably seem more just
and reasonable even than it does, were it not
for the fact that by this time the disease which
Emerson was concerned to cure has been
physicked into a worse and the patient so over-
dosed as to be completely disqualified for further
treatment of any kind. No one, I suppose,
would accuse us of a lack of self-confidence
nowadays. On the contrary, our fault appears
at first sight of just the opposite nature—over-
weeningness. Experience, example, expostulation are lost upon us. And our intellectual
insignificance is due, not to our subservience,
but to our distaste and disdain of any properly
constituted authority. Was there ever, I wonder, a time in which the opinion of the ignorant
and incompetent was allowed to impose itself
so freely in literature, politics, and morals, and
to debauch without check or protest the judgment of the entire public? If our current literature is thoroughly subdued to a vulgar and
uncultivated vogue, it is due to the public's

ignorance of tradition and its impatience of sound criticism. In fact, in our present temper it is next to impossible that such a thing as a constituted body of enlightened critical opinion on any subject should exist. On the one hand there is, in the case of literature, a number of writers of excellent parts who go astray for want of direction and restraint; on the other hand there is a vain and half-educated public persisting inveterately in its own bad sense, asserting as its highest critical canon that it knows what it likes, though no one would suppose so, to mark the fluctuations of its taste.

To be sure, for all our self-assertion there is at least one respect in which we are still notoriously in leading strings; what higher education we have is still largely under bonds to Germany. In that particular we are not yet emancipated or self-reliant by any means. The most prominent graduate school in the country is virtually a German university on American soil. Many of our professors, perhaps the better part of them, have been trained abroad and are now engaged in repeating to their countrymen what they have learned by rote of some foreigner. Not even their method is their own. On the whole the manner of instruction is a cross, and a very unhappy one, between the system of recitations and the system of lectures, combining the worst features of both; while perhaps the most incon-

gruous thing in the whole fantastic monument
of error is the inevitable graduate school, a
ridiculous and mischievous parasite in nine
cases out of ten, of which Dr. Jordan himself
says that it produces hardly a contribution to
knowledge of the slightest importance or one
valuable thesis out of a thousand. And, still
worse, what these foreign imitators are so
busily and thoughtlessly domesticating is an
ideal of education quite opposed to our traditions, needs, and temper—an education which
is monarchical, military, and beaurocratic; in
short, the ideal of imperial Prussia, not of re-
publican America. In fact, so great is the
confusion at present, so bewildered and uncertain our "educators," that they appear willing
to try any experiment—indeed, it is their ex-
perimenting which is accountable for much of
the muddle. For the very lack of that authoritative sense of the subject which leaves us to
imitate others, for the reason that we have no
standard of our own, is also the cause of the
perplexity and chaos into which we fall the
moment we attempt to assert our independence
and make a system for ourselves. Then our
efforts, just because they are revolutionary and
without restraint, become so wild and extravagant as to threaten the extinction of culture
altogether. And so it happens that where our
education is the most original, in the sense of

being most American, it is also most sordid and
material; for there it is least restrained by an
elevated ideal but is left to follow the vulgar
sense of the general public, which recognises no
standard of values except money and would
gladly turn the university into a mere professional school, a school of trades and utilities.

Nor is it difficult to trace the progress of the
demoralisation within the narrow limits of my
own experience. Not so very long ago there
was at least a small number of subjects in the
curriculum of every college or university which
served to give it a broad, if rather general,
moral basis. In those days life was still supposed to be a matter of conduct, not wholly
an affair of successful if unscrupulous money-
making and bread-winning. And those studies
were valued which were thought likely to form
character and supply correct motives of action.
But nowadays not only are the sciences suffered
to encroach upon these subjects, but the latter
themselves are no longer handled as moral
themes. Prominent among such lapsed branches
are history and literature. Properly taught,
history should be one of the most informing
studies in the course. But now that it has
come to posture as a methodology or a social,
industrial, economic interpretation, envious
of the name of science and curious rather of
documents and *paperasse* than of human life

and human nature, it has sacrificed almost all
its possible significance. And the same remark
is true of literature—not merely of English literature but of the literature of other languages
as well. In particular the classic literatures,
which contain the foundations of our culture,
were formerly looked upon as its necessary
buttresses. But now the classics, if they are
taught at all—for as a rule our classical faculties
are going in for football—have degenerated into
mere exercises in grammar or philology; while
our own literature, over which such an unintelligent clamour is rising these days, appears no
longer as a moral interpretation of life, as a
collection of human wisdom on the subject that
concerns us most to know, but as an ingenious
pretext for the study of linguistic derivations
and affiliations. In short our universities, while
pretending to prepare for life, are more and
more neglecting that in which life really consists—our education, like our civilisation, has
well-nigh ceased to be moral at all. And what
makes the matter even more desperate is the
fact that the successful "educator" is becoming
himself as unscrupulous as the education he
seeks to impart. He is no longer a scholar, a
man of reflection and contemplation, a moral
or at least an intellectual creature essentially.
He has become a man of business who turns
his department or his institution into a shop

and runs it like a commercial enterprise. He
is *affairé*, bustling, pretentious, not over-nice
in his transactions,—an advertiser, a showman,
and even something of a charlatan. In the face
of all this it is anything but reassuring to consider that upon the university devolves almost
exclusively the preservation of that permanent
tradition of human culture which alone enables
us to distinguish between worse and better,
between the things that are of but temporary
and secondary importance to us and those which
are of abiding worth and significance. Heaven
forbid that I should underrate the importance
of subsistence. But it is essential that we should
distinguish, that we should not confound the
accessory with the principal or set our hearts
upon things of transient concern as though they
were essential and of the first consequence. And
if our universities fail to assist in maintaining
this distinction and in fixing our hearts upon
the things that are essential, where shall we
find help to-day either for ourselves or for our
civilisation?

The Hindus have a beautiful apologue of life,
under the image of a dancing girl, who comes
out and exercises her art for a while before the
king. And for a while he watches her with
pleasure, till she finally retires, and he remains
sitting alone as before, satisfied with his own
thoughts and without regret now that the per-

formance is over and he is left by himself again. For after all the spectacle is [but for a little and is at best an illusion only. Sooner or later our material interests, our business and our money-getting, our little transactions of one kind or another, even our fads and hobbies—all these things which serve to occupy us for the moment, will fall away and leave us to ourselves without other assistance or support than that which we have within ourselves. And so I say, an education which does not furnish us with provision against that day, which does not provide us with comfort and sustainment against the inevitable collapse of life—such an education is a failure.

There is no chance and no anarchy in the universe. Every god is there sitting in his sphere. The young man enters the hall of the firmament; there is he alone with them alone, they pouring on him benedictions and gifts, and beckoning him up to their thrones. On the instant, and incessantly, fall snow-storms of illusions. He fancies himself in a vast crowd which sways this way and that and whose movements and doings he must obey; he fancies himself poor, orphaned, insignificant. The mad crowd drives hither and thither, now furiously commanding this thing to be done, now that. What is he that he should resist their will, and think or act for himself? Every moment new changes and new showers of deceptions to baffle and distract him. And when, by and by, for an instant, the air clears and the cloud lifts a little, there are the gods still sitting around him on their thrones,—they alone with him alone.

That, after all, in spite of ḥis momentary inconsistencies, is what Emerson means .by self-reliance—a confidence, not in our own whims and caprices, but in the permanent and essential interests of the spirit, a detachment from things of temporary and secondary account and an ability to bear their absence and loss, while resting in our sense of the great inalterable realities, which have been approved in the course of history by the witness of tradition, and which are commended ịn their application to the present emergency by the best judgment of our own day.

THE END